the Y2K

Survival Guide
and Cookbook

... recipes for woodstove, fireplace and campfire cooking, storing food and supplies, and getting ready for any emergency.

By Dorothy R. Bates and Albert K. Bates

Copyright © 1999 Dorothy R. Bates and Albert K. Bates
First Printing, January 1999
Second Printing, February 1999

Book Design, Cover and Illustrations by Albert K. Bates

Published by
ecovillage
a division of Global Village Institute
          PO Box 90
          Summertown TN 38483-0090
          931-964-3992
Printed in the United States of America

ecovillage® *is a registered trademark of Global Village Institute for Appropriate Technology. TVP® is a registered trademark of Archer Daniels Midland. iMac® is a registered trademark of Apple Computer, Inc. Girl Scouts® is a registered trademark of the Girl Scouts of the USA.*

02 00 99   5 4 3 2 1

Publisher's Cataloging-in-Publication
(Provided by Quality Books, Inc.)

Bates, Dorothy R., 1921-
    The Y2K survival guide and cookbook / by
Dorothy R. Bates and Albert K. Bates -- 1st ed.

    p. cm.
    Includes index.
    ISBN 0-96669317-0-X
    1. Survival and emergency rations. 2. Food --
Storage. 3. Emergency management. 4. Year 2000
date conversion (Computer systems)--Miscellanea.
I. Bates, Albert K., 1947-   II. Title.

TX601.B38 1999   641.4'8
                          QBI99-63

Dedication

This is dedicated to the hundreds of individuals who risked their careers, reputations and safety to put out the warning.

Acknowledgements

The authors wish to express profound gratitude to those who put information into the public domain to make research for our book as easy as it was. We especially acknowledge our indebtedness to the American Red Cross, the Girl Scouts of America, the U.S. Department of Agriculture, the Church of Jesus Christ Latter Day Saints (Mormons), the Southern Baptist Convention, and in no particular order, Art Bell, Edward Yardeni, Gary North, Robert Bennett, Eric Utne, Tom Atlee, Doc Childre, Bruce Cryer, Paloma O'Riley, Captain Dave, Michael S. Hyatt, Russ Kelly, Joel Ackerman, Dave Bettinger, Joe Boivin, Douglass Carmichael, Dennis Elenburg, Thierry Falissard, Karl Feilder, Alan Greenspan, Cory K. Hamasaki, Peter de Jager, Adam Kaplan, Leon Kappleman, Roleigh Martin, Scott Olmsted, Charles Reuben, Alan Simpson, Harlan Smith, Ed Yourdon, Nicholas Zvegintzov, the good people at y2ksupply.com, Mushroompeople and the Book Publishing Company, and many, many others.

This book was written and illustrated on an Apple iMac using Adobe PageMaker and Macromedia Freehand. The website for this project, y2k.ecovillage.org, was created using GoLive CyberStudio and Macromedia Flash. The typeface is Donata over Verdana.

Happiness belongs to the self-sufficient.

—Aristotle

CONTENTS

Coping with Catastrophe

F riday December 31st of 1999 marks not just the end of a day, a month, and a year but the end of a decade and of a century. At 12 o'clock midnight on January 1, the year 2000 and the new millennium begins.

But the question many people are asking is: when the clock strikes 12 will we find ourselves in 2000 or in 1900?

And as of this writing the very real possibility exists that hundreds of millions of software programs and embedded computer microchips will shut down the systems they are designed to control.

Urp!

The result could be rolling brownouts or total blackouts, as power companies scramble to find errant chips in power plants, transformer yards, and grid delivery systems. Computerized railroad switches could halt delivery of coal and oil, food and freight. For a few days, a few weeks, or even a few months, there might be problems with telephone service, water purification plants, sewage treatment plants, hospitals, banks, grocery stores, drug stores, gas stations, and public transportation. Office buildings, government agencies and Wall Street may have to shut down for an extended holiday if the goods they need and services they provide cannot be delivered.

Even if you have electricity or a backup generator, many home appliances, heating systems, and security systems may fail, because time-coded logic chips are involved in their operation. Even your automobile may have a computer controlling it!

The Millennium Bug

The problem with computers (even many PC's) is that while they can tell time to the billionth of a second they may not know what century it is. The Nuclear Regulatory Commission (NRC), whose primary function is enforcing safety at U.S. nuclear plants says: "... systems may misread the Year 2000 and cause the system to fail, generate faulty data, or act in an incorrect manner. The Y2K problem is urgent because it has a fixed nonnegotiable deadline that is quickly approaching."

The U.S. Senate has a Special Committee on the Year 2000 Technology Problem. So does the United Nations. Your local bank and your local electric company have committees, too. So far, these committees are *not promising to have solutions ready in time*.

Apocalypse Now?

Some analysts predict a turbulent time of social upheaval with starvation in some cities, no police force to protect people who stored food and water, a lack of health care, and a meltdown of civilization as we know it. Others predict a time of brownout, with isolated power failures, lasting a few weeks at most. Whom do we believe? After studying the matter for more than a year, the Chairman of the

United Nations Working Group on Informatics warned on
September 16, 1998:

> History offers no example of a parallel threat on a global, national or even lo-
> cal scale. To "wait and see" invites disaster. Only the long term threats of
> global warming, oxygen loss, exhaustion of other basic resources in the
> oceans and continents as well as the eventual possibility of an earth-asteroid
> collision demand worldwide action on a similar scale. And none of those
> problems present us with the Y2K date-positive threat, just months away... A
> worldwide strategic mobilization for Y2K contingency priorities similar to
> the effort required by World War II must be developed in the weeks ahead.

As we write this, a year before the big event, we are
significantly less pessimistic in our predictions. The computerized industrial world has enjoyed half a century of unparal-
leled prosperity. Most people in the West have a lot of resources to draw upon before their situation begins to ap-
proach even the present poverty of former Eastern Bloc
countries, where currency is often worthless, stores ration
basic commodities, and crime is rampant, but still people get
by, a decade after the Big Change. It could take substantially
longer for economies like the United States, Germany, or
Japan to sink to such levels. Within a few days of the loss of
electrical and communications utilities, assuming that were
to happen, national emergency measures could effect a
substantial recovery in the delivery of food, medical and
other basic services.

But even if the millennium bug turns out to be no big
deal, even just a false scare, making preparations is not a
bad thing to do. Serious and unexpected misfortune can
strike at any time. Tornadoes, hurricanes, ice storms, earthquakes, floods, droughts, fires, economic depressions,
hyperinflation, strikes, and civil unrest can happen to anyone. In 1998, a General Motors strike caused 200,000
workers to go without paychecks for 8 weeks. In Minnesota,
blizzards (with wind chill of -80 to -90°F) left people
stranded for weeks in their homes, some for days in their
vehicles on the highway before being found. Floods and
completely unpredictable mudslides from Bangladesh to
Honduras left tens of millions without homes. Earthquakes
and fires destroyed the life savings of many others. The
unimaginable can happen with unpredictable suddenness.

How do you get through a catastrophic time if it happens
to you? In a power blackout that lasts several weeks, the
shortage of water supplies and sewage plants can be a
greater threat to people's health than the shutdown of
doctors' offices and hospitals. Food may be worth more than
money. A kerosene lamp or stored water may be one of the
most valuable things you own.

Assessing your situation

The first step to becoming a survivor is finding out how vulnerable you are. Take a pad of paper and a pen or pencils. Physically go to every room in your house. Write down for each room:

- Every appliance and fixture (medical devices, sink, tub, mirror, light, window, heater, fan, vent, etc.).
- Everything else in the room (clothes, furniture, towels, medications, toothpaste, toilet brush, everything!).
- Everything in all the drawers, boxes, and storage containers.
- Every utility and service in the room (natural gas, electric, water, batteries, etc.).

Walk around the exterior of your house and note where all the utilities enter your home and where the shut off valves are. Note outside lights, security systems, sprinklers, propane tanks. Go through the garage, storage shed, under the porch, in the attic and crawl space, and write down everything you find, even the smallest items.

List the services you purchase regularly: newspaper delivery, garbage and recycling, grocery, laundry, transportation.

Brainstorm alternatives

Sit down with your lists and indicate which items are:

- Not essential (they are merely a convenience)
- Essential but not critical (you could get by without them for a few days)
- Critical (health and safety would be jeopardized without them)

Mark which items could not possibly work or be available if there was a loss of electricity, telecommunications, water or sanitation services. For all those marked or added to the at-risk category, you now need to find alternatives. Do this for all the items designated at risk.

Now you must do the research and find out if you can implement changes physically and financially. Don't rely on information from just one company. Talk to several, get brochures, talk to hardware stores, search the web. The best solution may be the simplest. Low-tech also means low repairs and low replacement.

Implement

As you implement your alternatives, make sure you keep all manuals and warranties, learn how to use each tool properly and how to fix what you install, and always keep spare parts and repair tools on hand.

Gather—for everyone in your home—any information that may be needed in an emergency. Include the following:

- List all medications, over the counter and prescription, that all family members use. Don't forget emergency items such as medication for allergic reactions to bee stings.
- List any supplies used with them, such as needles, alcohol swabs, lancets, etc.
- List all medical conditions, allergies, predispositions, surgeries, etc.
- List all devices used at home or at a medical facility (e.g. dialysis machine, pacemaker, glucose testing equipment, inhalers, respirators, etc.).

Discuss with your doctor:

- How to order enough medication and supplies in advance and store them safely.
- How to handle medical conditions in an emergency. Do you need to purchase additional equipment, or get training?

Find out from the manufacturers of the devices if they will work without error through the date change. Also, find out from your doctor what you can do if the device doesn't work properly or fails. There may be alternatives you can use in an emergency.

Make sure all the equipment you use has spare parts, and that you know how to fix them, and have the proper tools on hand. Practice fixing equipment, and test any emergency plans and training.

Try to schedule needed exams, tests, etc., with results returned well before the end of 1999. If your doctor has not paid attention to the Y2K problem, he may "misplace" your medical records. Get hard copies of your medical file, x-rays, etc. to keep at home.

Take an advanced first aid class, CPR, etc. Learn especially how to tell the difference between life threatening or non-life threatening conditions. When in doubt, however, always err on the side of caution. Learning how to deal with such situations yourself will reduce the likelihood of panic, and increase the chances of survival for the ill or injured person.

If ambulances can't be contacted, you'll need to transport the person yourself, properly and safely. Make sure you know the location of the nearest emergency facilities, and try to contact them before you go. Check with such places before the turn of the century to see what their contingency plans are in the event ambulance services fail, emergency personnel are unavailable, or communications and power failures happen.

Remember, don't expect the same quality of care you are used to if there is a general emergency in your community. Try to help out, and don't demand immediate treatment.

Basic Needs

Wastewater and sewage treatment facilities are highly automated and environmental emissions monitoring and control systems depend on year-2000-vulnerable embedded controls. Malfunctions due to year 2000 problems could lead to polluting releases and emissions that could endanger local residents. Be wary of tap water and "gray" water used for outside purposes. Home water testing kits can help you check. The best defense is a store of emergency water.

Most of us buy our food at supermarkets. If there is a breakdown in the supply chain, we could experience shortages or store closures. The best alternative is, of course, buying what you need ahead of time. Start by laying in nonperishable basics today, such as toilet tissue, bleach, and dry and canned goods.

The cheapest way to purchase goods is by case-lot. It's not always easy to find, but talk to the managers of your favorite store, and see if they'll sell to you in bulk. Look for Farmers' Markets or join a food co-op.

Don't allow garbage to accumulate outside your home. In some rural areas, trash can be particularly attractive to a variety of wildlife—some dangerous. If waste builds up, dig a trench and bury it.

The greatest concern in an emergency is reaching someone who can help. If the phone lines are down, you might be able to reach emergency services by CB. However, even if phones work, there's no guarantee that the machines and equipment emergency personnel use will work, and correctly. That leaves it up to you.

Keep Hard Copies of all Financial Papers

- Bank statements, cancelled checks, check stubs
- Paid bills, expense receipts
- Charitable contribution receipts
- Medical bills and receipts
- Brokerage confirmation slips, statements
- Property tax receipts, records of mortgage payments
- Business records (partnerships or buy-sell agreements)
- Insurance policies
- Income Tax returns

If you have no written confirmation (like cancelled checks and mortgage coupons) write letters to everyone who has recently received payments, or who owes you money. Ask them to supply written documentation of the account to date. This applies to: IRS, Social Security, VA, Banks, Stockbrokers, Mortgage and Insurance Companies, Credit Card Issuers, Doctors, Hospitals and Local Tax authorities.

Do not count on your bills, mortgage, etc., being paid for you if you have automatic payment. Pay them manually at least 3-4 months in advance, for a 2 month period, extending into February of 2000. Make sure you keep track of all payments and have hardcopy receipts. If there's a problem, it'll be up to you to prove you made the payment. Be especially alert to document quarterly IRS payments.

If there are penalties associated with pre- or advance payments, discuss this with your creditor. Ask if they will waive penalty fees even if only for a few months. If they won't, try to work out an agreement of suspending any late fee penalties if automatic payments fail to work. Get any and all agreements in writing.

Cash is often the best exchange in an emergency. Checks, credit cards, and debit cards may be useless. Put any cash, preferably in small bills, in a safe place in a non-obvious, readily-accessible location.

Expect prices to go up, especially if there are shortages of any goods like food or water. Inflation is caused by many things—not the least of which is greed. Make sure you know more than one source to purchase goods, and that they are reliable. However, do expect there to be shortages and plan accordingly.

Mass Hysteria the Greatest Threat

In any large scale crisis, we have more to fear from mass hysteria than from any actual shortages. Even banks which have their computer systems Y2K ready would have to shut their doors if a multitude of customers line up for cash. While the U.S. government has printed billions of extra dollars in anticipation of heavy demand in late 1999, lack of secure storage space meant they could not print more than a small percent of the total dollars on deposit. Everyone's money is safe, and insured. It just can't all be used at once.

Gather a Group

Instead of trying to prepare for the millennium challenges all by yourself, get together with your neighbors to discuss preparation. Call an apartment floor meeting or a block party on your street. You may want to elect a committee to come up with a plan. You may want to take advantage of the low prices of buying food in bulk as members of a group.

A number of Y2K books talk about "bug out" strategies or stockpiling guns, ammunition and gold coins. Frankly, none of those preparations are very practical. The two of us have been to Russia on several occasions and have seen the practice of city-dwellers renting garden space an hour or two out into the country. Having a secure food supply is a good precaution, but most of what city-dwellers need to survive is right in the city. The rural countryside can be very inhospitable to intruders, and is likely to be the *last* place that utilities and government services will be restored after a major interruption.

The best security is a prepared neighbor. Talk to your neighbors. You don't have to convince them Y2K is a problem. Merely explain that it's something you're concerned about. Let them know that you are preparing, and if they wish to talk about it, they're welcome to talk to you any time.

If several neighbors become interested, then start holding regular meetings. Discuss some of the problems Y2K may cause and how you can pull together to handle them, and how you can share resources to help those of you who are physically or financially disadvantaged.

One swimming pool stores enough water for many people to have cleansing baths for an extended time. Tools such as chainsaws and outdoor barbecues can serve many households. By sharing and cooperating, everyone in the neighborhood will have an easier time.

Get Together Recipes

Cheeseless Macaroni
6 servings

8 ounces elbow macaroni
2 quarts boiling water
1 teaspoon salt
3 cups nutritional yeast sauce
1/2 cup cracker crumbs

Cook pasta in boiling water until tender. Drain, save water for soup. Mix pasta and sauce, put in baking dish, top with cracker crumbs. Bake at 350° for 30 minutes. Cut in squares to serve.

Nutritional Yeast Sauce
about 3 cups

1/2 cup white flour
1/2 cup Nutritional Yeast (cheese substitute: 1-800-695-2241)
1/2 cup canola oil
3 cups water
1 teaspoon salt

In a heavy pan, heat flour and yeast until you can almost smell it (about 3-4 minutes). Pour in oil, stir in water and salt. Cook until thick and bubbly.

Spaghetti Marinara
4 to 6 servings

1 Tablespoon olive oil
1 medium onion, chopped small
1 medium carrot, minced
1 clove garlic, minced
1 28 oz. can plum tomatoes, diced
1 teaspoon dried basil
1 teaspoon dried oregano
Salt and pepper to taste
1 pound thin spaghetti, cooked, drained

Heat pan, add oil and onion and carrot, cook until onion is soft. Add garlic and tomatoes, bring to a boil, taste for salt and pepper. Toss sauce with pasta.

Organizing Neighbors

1. Get acquainted with the neighbors. Attend yard sales, or give one; borrow a cup of sugar, or offer a cup of coffee; organize a block party, or pass a petition. Express your concerns.

2. Convene meetings to brainstorm and plan strategy, inventory neighborhood resources and offer mutual support. Get a volunteer to take minutes of the meeting, and offer

notepaper for anyone who might want to take personal notes.

Begin the meeting by introducing yourself and explaining your purpose in calling the meeting. Then have each person introduce him or herself, with a bit of personal background and expression of personal concerns about Y2K. It's important, too, to have each one offer whatever resources, expertise, or services he or she may be willing to contribute and to express his or her expectations of the group.

Once all concerns have been expressed, have the note-taker summarize the specific areas of uncertainty or insecurity, and the specific offerings of individuals. Discuss what else might be necessary to satisfy neighborhood needs: more information regarding risks, or business and community preparations underway; equipment, tools or materials lacking; communications with other neighborhood groups. Compose a list of all such needs, and get each person to commit to contributing or participating in some constructive way. Assign individual roles and "homework."

Your group must decide what measures to take on as a team effort, and which are to be left to individual households, or to utility companies, businesses, government agencies or charities.

3. Offer your services to the local Police, Fire and Emergency Services. You can assist by helping to raise funds for new equipment, alternative and/or backup energy and communication sources, etc. Get several neighbors together and go speak at city council meetings, public hearings and other functions.

Many people who prepare for Y2K are labeled as survivalists, alarmists or worse. Critics blur the difference between taking prudent precautions and extreme lifestyle changes.

Those who prepare for the possibility of catastrophe will have a much easier time surviving it. And today is the day you begin to prepare, not after the mass hysteria develops, long lines begin to form, and shelves are empty.

If you see a bandwagon, it's too late.
—Sir James Goldsmith

The greatest antidote to worry, whether you're getting ready for a space flight or facing a problem of daily life, is preparation. The more you prepare, the more you study, the more you think, the more you try to envision what might happen and what your best response and options are, the more you are able to allay your fears about the future...

Obviously, there's a limit to how well you can prepare for everything, because our lives are continually made up of unforeseen events. That's why I stressed so much to my own children the value of education—this encapsulated experience of everyone who has lived before us. It enabled them to have as much preparation as possible for the unknowns that are in the future for all of us.

—Senator John Glenn, 25 Oct 1998

Step 1.
What To Do in Any Emergency

Weeks ahead of Y2K day, you can survey the contents of your medicine cabinet and check basic supplies. Items to have on hand include:

Ace Bandage - in case of sprains
Acetaminophen or Ibuprofen or both, for aches, colds, fevers or flu
Antacids for heartburn
Adhesive bandages, gauze pads, adhesive tape
Allergy pills or antihistamines
An aloe plant or ointment for burns
Aspirin
Bacitracin, Neosporin, or other antibiotic salve
Calamine lotion for poison ivy
Cold relief pills
Cough drops and/or cough syrup
Corn plasters
Decongestants
Eye drops
Hydrogen Peroxide
Iodine
Lip balm

Petroleum jelly
Snake bite kit
Sun screen
Sanitary napkins or tampons
Thermometer

Add to your list if anyone in the family ever has need of remedies for:

Athlete's foot
Asthma
Constipation
Diarrhea
Hemorrhoids
Denture adhesive
Ear aches
Lice
Incontinence
PMS
Dry skin
Tooth aches
Bladder infections
Birth control
Depression

Provide the appropriate remedy where possible. Talk to your doctor about any prescription drugs a family member takes regularly. Try to have a three-month supply on hand.

Invest in a good supply of **multivitamin pills** of a kind preferred by each member of the family, i.e. chewables for little ones, etc.

Especially have on hand a *Book of Home Remedies.*

FIRE

Fire is the most common disaster affecting people. Each year, thousands of our neighbors are left homeless by fires which may affect only one home or hundreds.

You should check your home and place of business regularly, following the fire department's suggestions for fire prevention.

If fire does occur, you should know what to do, how to escape, how to safeguard your family, yourself and your co-workers.

- Have a plan. Make sure you know how to get out in case of fire — and what to do if your planned exit is blocked by flames. Every person should know the plan.
- Don't panic. Having a plan guards against panic.
- Call the fire department. Don't try to fight the fire yourself. Make sure everyone knows how to call the fire department.
- Don't use elevators. In a high-rise apartment or office building, use stairways or fire escapes. Fire could burn through electrical wiring and leave you trapped in an elevator.
- Close doors. A closed door will hold back the fire and keep out poisonous smoke until the fire department can rescue you.
- Feel for heat with the back of your hand. Don't open any door until you have felt it, especially near the top, for heat. If it's hot, don't open it.
- Smoke and heat rise to the ceiling and bank downward. There is an area 12 to 18 inches from the floor containing clean air to breathe while you make your way out.
- Find good air. If you cannot escape, stay near the floor, where the air is better. If all doors are closed, open a window for air. If possible, stuff wet rags around doors to hold back smoke and heat.
- Signal for help. If you are trapped, signal with a flashlight or light-colored sheet or towel.
- Get together. As part of your plan, have a common meeting spot outside where your family will assemble. Count people as they arrive.
- Stay out. Do not, for any reason, go back into a burning building. If someone is missing, tell the firefighters.
- Always call 911 to report a fire and call from a neighbor's house.
- Don't try to call and report the fire before you get out.

ABOVE ALL, DON'T PANIC
The fire department is only minutes away.

EARTHQUAKE

The actual movement of the ground in an earthquake is seldom the direct cause of death and injury. Most casualties result from falling objects and debris. Earthquakes also may trigger landslides and generate huge ocean waves, each of which can cause great damage. There are many actions which you can take to reduce the dangers to yourself, your family, and others.

Before an Earthquake Occurs....

1. Check your home for hazards.

2. Hold family earthquake drills and plan for reunification.

3. Teach responsible family members how to turn off utilities at main switches and valves.

4. Take first aid training.

5. Keep immunizations and medications up to date.

6. Gather together supplies and medications which will allow your family to survive for at least 72 hours (food, water, clothing).

7. Make an outdoor cache. In any major disaster, emergency government services may be temporarily overwhelmed. A section of large drainage pipe, sealed on both ends, can be buried in the back yard and made watertight. If the house burns down or is carried away, this cache can provide a short term supply of dry and canned food, tools, clothes, and other necessities.

8. Have a crescent or pipe wrench on hand to turn off gas and water. Keep flashlights and batteries in several locations in case of a power failure.

During an Earthquake....

1. Stay calm.

2. Inside, stand in a doorway or crouch under a desk or table, away from windows. Watch for falling objects.

3. Outdoors, stand away from buildings, trees, telephone, and electrical lines.

4. On the road, drive away from underpasses/overpasses. Stop in a safe area. Stay in your vehicle.

After an Earthquake...

1. Check for injuries. Provide first aid.

2. Check for gas, water, sewage breaks and for downed electrical lines and shorts. Turn off appropriate utilities. Check for building damage and potential safety problems.

3. Wear shoes.

4. Clean up dangerous spills.

5. Turn on radio and listen for instructions from public safety agencies.

6. Don't use the telephone except for emergencies.

FLOODS AND HURRICANES

Floods and hurricanes usually have good advance warning. Know the maximum storm surge that might occur. If you are in an area that should evacuate, do so, the sooner the better. If you stay, secure the area for broken glass and rising water. Remove items that might blow down or away in high winds, like TV antennas.

Brace your garage door. Garbage cans, awnings, loose garden tools, toys, and other loose objects can be deadly missiles. Anchor them securely or bring them indoors. Cover windows and other glass. Board up or shutter large windows securely. Tape exposed glass to minimize shattering. Draw draperies across large windows and doors to protect against flying glass if shattering does occur.

Store valuables and important papers. Put irreplaceable documents in waterproof containers and store them in the highest possible spot. If you evacuate, be sure to take them with you.

Here is a quick grocery list to get you through a few days of isolation:

Bread, crackers
Peanut butter and jelly
Cookies and snacks
Apples, bananas, oranges and other fresh fruit
Applesauce and canned fruit
Raisins and other dried fruit
Beverages in cans or boxes
Fruit drinks; milk products that don't require refrigeration
Plastic eating utensils, paper plates and napkins
Baby food, diapers, formula, and sterile water
Bottled water, ice
Charcoal, matches
Toilet paper, paper towels and pre-moistened towelettes
Pet food
Garbage bags

When rising water threatens your home, move everything you can to the upper floors or to a place of safety on high ground. Local authorities will help you evacuate if there is time. If you have no place to go, there will be public shelters. Disconnect electrical appliances and move small appliances and motors in large ones to safety. Turn off the main electrical switch and cover the electrical outlets with tape before leaving. Tape freezer and refrigerator shut. Take with you important papers, eyeglasses, false teeth, prescription medicines—things you may need while you are out of your house.

If the water is rising rapidly during or after heavy rains, don't wait to make preparations. Move your family to high ground immediately. Flash floods will rise faster than you think and cut off your escape. If you are driving in a flood area and your car is stalled by rising water, leave it immediately and wade back to high ground.

If you are trapped in a car that goes under water, you can get out of the submerged vehicle by opening a window or door and swimming to safety. While you're preparing to get out, move to the highest part of the car to breathe any air that is trapped there.

If you live at the shore, never let your vehicle gas tank be less than half-full during hurricane season; fill up as a hurricane watch is posted. Remember: When there is no electricity, gas pumps won't work. Make sure you have some cash. Remember that automated teller machines also won't work without electricity.

Secure your boat. Move boats on trailers close to your house and fill with water to weigh them down. Lash securely to trailer and use tie-downs to anchor the trailer to the ground or house. Double mooring lines of boats in the water, and then leave them. Double lash-down canvas, remove loose gear, and close seacocks.

If considering moving to a shelter, make arrangements for all pets. Do not leave them unattended. Pets are not allowed in shelters. Lock windows and doors. Turn off your gas, water, and electricity. Take food and water.

When a flood is over, don't return home until authorities say it is safe. Beware of outdoor hazards. Watch out for loose or dangling power lines, and report them immediately to local officials. Many lives are lost to electrocution. Walk or drive cautiously, as debris-filled streets are dangerous. Snakes and poisonous insects may be a hazard. Washouts may weaken roads and bridges, which could collapse under vehicle weight.

Don't drink the water from a faucet unless it is announced that it is all right to do so. Don't turn on any electrical appliances until they have been checked. If you smell escaping gas, report it immediately. And don't use any food that has been in a freezer or refrigerator if the power was off for a long period of time. Freezers will keep foods several days if doors are not opened after power failure, but do not refreeze food once it begins to thaw.

Take extra precautions to prevent fires. Lower water pressure in city and town water mains and the interruption of other services may make fire fighting extremely difficult after a hurricane or flood.

MUDSLIDES AND AVALANCHE

Sudden mudslides gushing down rain-sodden slopes and gullies are widely recognized by geologists as a hazard to human life and property. Most mudslides are localized in small gullies, threatening only those buildings in their direct path. They can burst out of the soil on almost any rain-saturated hill when rainfall is heavy enough. Often they occur without warning in localities where they have never been seen before.

Ashy slopes left denuded by wildfires are especially susceptible to mudslides during and immediately after major rainstorms. Those who live downslope of a wildfire area should be aware of this potential for slope failure that is present until new vegetation rebinds the soil.

Debris avalanches and debris flows are shallow landslides, saturated with water, that travel rapidly downslope as muddy or snowy slurries. The flowing mud or snow carries rocks, bushes, and other debris as it pours down the slopes.

Speeds in excess of 20 mph are not uncommon, and speeds in excess of 100 mph, although rare, do occur. Houses in the path of debris avalanches can be demolished. Persons in these structures can be severely injured or killed.

Most rainstorms are of such low intensity that they do not trigger debris avalanches. Some intense storms may trigger only a few debris avalanches. However, when the ground is already saturated from previous rain, even relatively short high-intensity rainstorms may trigger debris avalanches. For example, in January 1982, an intense rainstorm triggered literally tens of thousands of debris avalanches in the San Francisco Bay area. Mudslides were responsible for most of the casualties of Hurricane Mitch in 1998.

Debris avalanches occur all over the world. They are particularly common in mountainous areas underlain by rocks that produce sandy soils. Debris flows are known to start on slopes as low as 15 degrees, but the more dangerous, faster moving flows (debris avalanches) are more likely to develop on steeper slopes. About two-thirds of all debris avalanches start in hollows or troughs at the heads of small drainage courses. Typically, a debris avalanche bursts out of a hillside and flows quickly downslope, inundating anything in its path. Because the path of a debris flow is controlled by the local topography just like flowing water, debris avalanches and debris flows generally follow stream courses.

Avoid building sites at the bottoms and mouths of steep ravines and drainage courses. These areas are the most likely to be inundated by debris flows. The outer "banks" of bends along such ravines also should be avoided because swiftly flowing debris avalanches can "ride up" out of the bottom of the stream channel where it bends.

Avoid building on or below steep slopes. In general, the steeper the slope the greater the risk. If these areas must be used, consult with a soils engineer and an engineering geologist. If steep cuts or fills occur below the discharge points of runoff water from streets, downspouts, or similar drainage facilities onto a slope, it may be wise to obtain expert advice.

Methods to reduce the hazard from debris avalanches include construction of a) deflection walls and b) debris fences. Because of the extreme force of impact associated with debris flows, these and similar structures should be carefully engineered and constructed.

Residents living directly downslope of mountainous wildfire areas should be aware that, in addition to life-threatening potential debris flows and other forms of mass movement, there is another, perhaps deadlier hazard—debris flooding or mud flooding at and near the mouths of channels that drain burned-over, ashy slopes. Studies have shown that, in the first year following a wildfire, sediment yields and peak discharges or such streams can increase up to 35-fold.

Before and during rains, frequent inspection of the slopes (above vulnerable sites) for extension cracks and other symptoms of downslope movements of slope materials can be a guide to impending failure and a warning to evacuate. In particular, watch for new springs or seeps on slopes; cracks in snow, ice, soil, or rock; bulges at the base of slopes; the appearance of holes or bare spots on hillsides; tilting trees; or increased muddiness of streams. Any sudden increase in runoff is cause for concern. Listen for unusual rumbling sounds or noises that may indicate shifting bedrock or breaking vegetation or structures.

Stay alert to the amount of rain falling locally during intense rainstorms. Buy a rain gauge (an inexpensive plastic one will suffice) and install it where it can be checked frequently. Whenever rainfall has exceeded 3 or 4 inches per day or 1 inch per hour, the soil may be waterlogged and more rain can trigger mudflows.

The single most important action that should be taken by residents on rainy nights is not to sleep in lower-floor bedrooms on the sides of houses that face hazardous slopes.

If venturing into snow areas where avalanche potential is present, carry an EPIRB signal device. If caught in an avalanche, cover your face and try to make a pocket of air. If you can be found within 20 minutes of burial, you should have enough air to survive.

AIRPLANE CRASHES

There are few predictive rules about surviving a plane crash. Sitting in front, at the wings, or in the rear confer no relative advantage because each crash is unique. An aisle seat may provide some advantage over a window seat.

Hyperventilate in the final moments before impact. The additional air in your lungs will give you added time to find an exit amid smoke and fire. When exiting, stay low. Many fatalities in air crashes are caused by inhaling toxic fumes.

Cover and pad yourself as much as possible. If you have a blanket or coat, put it over your head.

If you escape a crash, first render aid to the other survivors and then attempt to attract help.

Orienteering

If you find yourself in unfamiliar surroundings with no nearby roads, you can usually find civilization by walking downhill and downstream. Negotiating unknown territory at night can be very dangerous, but may be necessary in an emergency, or there are circumstances—in the desert for instance—when it may be more comfortable to travel at night.

The night is never completely dark and vision is not totally lost. However, because it is difficult to see things clearly, you are easily disoriented, which leads to a feeling of being lost. It is always darker among trees than out in the open - so keep to open country if you can. A compass is a great help in maintaining a heading, but you can also orient yourself in darkness by looking at the moon. If the moon rises before the sun has set, the illuminated side will be on the west. If the moon rises after midnight, the illuminated side will be in the east.

TORNADO

When a tornado approaches, your immediate action may mean life or death!

Seek inside shelter... stay away from windows... Keep your transistor radio tuned for the latest information.

- At home — The basement is best, under a heavy table or work-bench. If you have no basement, stay under heavy furniture in the center part of house. Keep windows open, but stay away from them.
- Mobile home — Get out! Find shelter in a sturdy building nearby. Mobile homes are tornado magnets.
- Office building —Interior hallway on a lower floor or preferably in the basement.
- Factory — Have a plan to move workers out of areas with wide unsupported roofs. Move to areas where there are good walls, such as hallways, or rest rooms.
- School — Move to interior hallways on the lowest floor. Avoid gymnasiums or other areas with a wide unsupported roof.
- Open country — Lie flat in ditch, ravine, or culvert. Move at right angles to the approaching funnel.

Do not call the Weather Service except to report a tornado.

WINTER STORMS

Become independent. Check battery-powered equipment, heating fuel, food stock, stored water and other supplies.

Dress for the season. Layers of protective clothing are more effective and efficient then single layers of thick cloth-ing. Mittens are warmer than gloves. Hoods or scarves should cover the mouth, to protect lungs from extremely cold air.

Keep a full set of cold weather clothing in waterproof packaging in the basement and in each car. Thermal under-wear, heavy shirts and pants, boots with extra liners, gloves, socks, hats, facemasks. Include an assortment of blankets and sleeping bags.

Don't exhaust yourself shoveling snow. It is extremely hard work and can bring on a heart attack, a major cause of death during and after winter storms.

Take winter driving seriously. Keep your car "winterized." Carry a winter car kit containing equipment such as blanket, water, etc. to help yourself keep warm, visible, and alive if you are trapped in a winter storm. Think a cellular phone is the answer? Sorry, the cell antennas require power to pick up your call and pass it on. And a cell phone will only reach a couple of miles.

If a blizzard traps you, avoid overexertion and exposure, stay in your vehicle (but keep it ventilated), exercise, turn on dome light at night, stand watches, and don't panic.

The body's largest organ, the skin, often suffers during the cold, dry winter months, but simple steps can prevent and alleviate dry skin. The key is to block in moisture and keep the barrier function of the skin intact. Older adults and anyone with sensitive skin are more prone to dryness. Over-the-counter, generic moisturizers are an effective preventative. Decrease showering and bathing to not more than every other day. Avoid hot water bathing. Switch to a mild, moisturizing soap from deodorant soap. Apply lotion throughout the day. Use a heavier cream or ointment at bedtime.

IF YOU ARE A DISASTER VICTIM

If a fire, flood, earthquake or any other kind of disaster leaves you and your family in need of emergency food, clothing or shelter, call your nearest Red Cross chapter. All Red Cross disaster assistance is an outright gift made possible by voluntary contributions.

A section on basic first aid appears in the back.

HOME SAFETY TIPS

- Keep stove and sink areas well lighted.
- Turn pot handles away from front of stove but not over another burner.
- Wipe up spilled grease or fluids immediately.
- Cut away from you when using a knife, and keep knives in rack or drawer compartment.
- Dry hands before using electrical appliances and never use such appliance while in bathtub.
- Use a stepstool to reach high cupboards.
- Have cracked or frayed electrical cords replaced by an electrician.
- Avoid wearing loose clothing around fire and don't use hairsprays near a flame or while smoking.
- Screen fireplaces.
- Use large, deep ashtrays and never smoke in bed or when you're likely to doze off.
- Keep insecticides, disinfectants, household cleaners, and medicines in original, clearly labeled containers and out of reach of children.
- Keep list of emergency telephone numbers —doctor, police, fire,

utilities, ambulance service, rescue squad, poison control center — near telephone.

- Keep walking areas and door entries clear of obstructions and tripping hazards. Have non-skid backing on small rugs and keep such rugs away from heads of stairs. Keep heavy traffic areas well lighted.

- Avoid carrying loads that block your vision.

- Keep stairs clear of toys and other stumbling blocks, and keep them well lighted at top and bottom. Keep treads and carpeting in good repair.

- Have sturdy handrails, indoors and on porches, and sturdy banisters on open stairs and stairwells.

- Equip tubs and showers with nonskid mats or textured surfaces and sturdy handbars, and keep nonskid bathrugs in front of tubs and showers.

- Keep night lights in bathrooms for elderly persons and children.

- Clean up floor spills and debris quickly.

- Keep extra records of all your important documents at a secure second location: include bank records, title deeds, insurance policies, and stock certificates.

Preparing for Y2K is the same as preparing for anything else—a little common sense goes a long way. The difference with Y2K is that it has a date which is known well in advance to millions of people. Some of them will "get it" early and buy what they need long before shortages appear and prices go up. Others will procrastinate or ignore the warning signs until it is too late to find even the simplest things, like candles and matches.

We hope by publishing this information a year ahead of the Big Event we will raise enough awareness that preparations can unfold in an orderly way, and everyone who wants to be is ready for whatever may come.

If it weren't for the last minute, a lot of things wouldn't get done.
—Michael B. Taylor

"The future of civilization depends on water. I beg you all to understand this."

—Jacques Yves Cousteau.

Step 2. Water

During starvation an animal can live if it loses nearly all the glycogen and fat, as well as half its body protein, but a loss of 20 percent of the water in the body results in death. A person can live without food for over a month, but without water only a few days. Since the human body is about 65 percent water we must consider it an important nutrient.

Water should be the first and most important item to stockpile. If we follow the recommendations that each person drink 8 glasses of water a day, that's 8 times 8 ounces or 64 ounces per person, or two quarts of water per person per day for drinking.

Allow an equal amount for cooking, brushing teeth and minimum cleaning up and you need:

4 quarts or one gallon of water per person per day.

For 2 persons, 2 gallons. For a family of 4, 4 gallons are needed. For a 3-day weekend, the family of 4 needs 12 gallons. For 30 days, a family of 4 would need 120 gallons! And this is rationing the amount of water used at all times. No flushing of toilets or washing of clothes is included in calculating minimum water needs.

In opaque, airtight containers, bacteria-free tap water can be kept indefinitely. The key question is, is it clean? To be safe, both the container AND its contents should be disinfected before storage begins. In storage, it should be tightly sealed, kept in a dark area, and it should be taste-tested every six months. Water properly stored can remain fresh for several years.

Save Empty Jugs Now

Don't discard any half-gallon or gallon jugs this year. Wash them well, rinse them with a solution of 1 Tablespoon bleach to a gallon of water, replace the clean cap and save the jugs to fill with fresh water. Jugs can be stored in a basement, garage or outdoors. If stored outdoors, they should be covered, because sunlight will embrittle plastic over time.

If you store water jugs outdoors and they are likely to freeze, fill the jugs only 4/5ths full, allowing room for ice to expand and not split the sides.

Add ascorbic acid powder to stored water as a preservative. Just 1/2 of a teaspoon (approximately 2 grams or 2,000 milligrams) added to a 2 quart jar of water may give a very faintly lemon flavor but the water will be healthier. Vitamin C or pure ascorbic acid soluble crystals can be obtained from Bronson Pharmaceuticals, La Canada, California, 91011.

Mark the date the jug was filled with a magic marker. Use the oldest water first.

Soft Drink Bottles

Two- and Three-liter soft drink bottles are ideal for water storage, but because they are clear plastic, water quality may deteriorate sooner.

Containers **NOT** to be used are those which retain strong odors, held toxic materials, or are made from biodegradable plastics, such as milk and distilled water containers. Biodegradable plastics will break down in about six months.

Disinfecting Water

In an emergency, river, lake and pond water might be seen as possible sources of water, but it must first be disinfected. Disinfectants are less effective for cloudy water. Filtering murky or colored water through clean cloths may produce sediment-free water suitable for disinfecting.

There are two general methods for disinfecting water, *boiling for 1 to 2 minutes,* or *chemical treatment.* Boiling will make water bacterially safe, chemical treatment will remove most pathogens.

Vigorous boiling for one minute will kill any disease-causing microorganism in water. The flat taste of boiled water

can be improved by aeration (pouring it back and forth between two containers), by allowing it to stand for a few
hours in a clean container, or by adding a pinch of salt for
each quart boiled.

Any water to be used for drinking, cooking, brushing teeth or any
other internal use should be properly disinfected.

When boiling is impractical, chemicals are commonly
used, as follows...

Chlorine Bleach

Common household bleach contains a chlorine compound
that will disinfect water. If no procedure is written on the label of the bleach container, find the percentage of available
chlorine and use the following table as a guide:

Available chlorine	Drops per quart of water
1%	10
4-6%	2
7-10%	1

If the strength is unknown, add ten drops to each quart.
Double this amount if the water is cloudy. The treated water
should be mixed thoroughly and allowed to stand for 30 minutes. A simple test of effectiveness is to take a small taste.
If the water doesn't taste of chlorine, repeat the dosage and
let it stand another 15 minutes. Standing longer in an open
container, or aerating by pouring back and forth will allow
much of the chlorine to off-gas and will reduce the chlorine
taste. You can do this after you know the water is free of
bacteria.

Granular Calcium Hypochlorite

One heaping teaspoon of Calcium Hypochlorite (approximately 1/4 ounce) dissolved in 2 gallons of water will produce a stock chlorine solution (500 mg/l), since Calcium Hypochlorite is about 70% chlorine.

Disinfected water should have a chlorination of 1 part
chlorine to 100 parts of water. That's 1 pint (16 oz.) of stock
chlorine to 12.5 gallons of water. **Don't confuse concentrated
Calcium Hypochlorite with stock chlorine!** A gallon of drinkable
water should have no more than a hundredth of an ounce of
Calcium Hypochlorite.

WATER BALANCE

(Average Individual)

Water Intake
Liquid Food 4.7 cups
Solid Food 2.1 – 3.8 cups
Water produced in body 1.7 cups
TOTAL 8.5 – 10.2 cups

Water Output
Vaporization (lungs & skin) 3.6 – 4.2 cups
Feces 0.3 – 0.4 cups
Urine 4.2 – 5.5 cups
TOTAL 8.4 – 10.1 cups

Chlorine Tablets

Chlorine tablets ready for disinfecting water can be pur-chased in prepared form with mixing instructions. When in-structions are not available, try one tablet for each quart of water and use the taste test.

Tincture of Iodine

If no chlorine is available, Iodine can be used. Iodine is not as helpful as chlorine, because it is ineffective against some pathogens, like Giardia or Cryptosporidium. It is best just to use iodine to disinfect wellwater, rather than surface water, because wellwater is less likely to have these organ-isms.

Common household iodine from the medicine chest or first aid kit is 2% iodine. Five drops should be added to each quart of clear water, 10 drops to each quart of cloudy water. Let stand for at least 30 minutes.

Iodine Tablets

Iodine water purification tablets can be found in most drug or sporting goods stores. When instructions are not available, use one tablet for each quart of water.

Rainwater

If you have a house with gutters, begin to collect rainwa-ter. (Grandmother Helen loved the softness of rainwater for washing her hair, and we always had a barrel, topped with some screening to keep out leaves, standing under eaves near the gutter downspout). Rainwater is so superior to

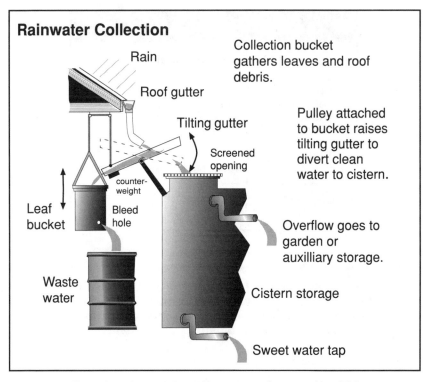

Rainwater Collection

Rain

Roof gutter

Collection bucket gathers leaves and roof debris.

Tilting gutter

Screened opening

Pulley attached to bucket raises tilting gutter to divert clean water to cistern.

counter-weight

Leaf bucket

Bleed hole

Overflow goes to garden or auxilliary storage.

Waste water

Cistern storage

Sweet water tap

most well and spring water that every home should have a supply. It requires no "softener," uses less soap and is friendlier to work with than even the best water that has come into contact with the ground.

A large heavy-duty plastic trash can with a hole cut into the lid can be placed under the drain pipe of your gutter to collect water. Cut some fine mesh screen and fasten under the hole to keep debris out. A simple system for dumping the leaves and dirt that collect on a roof before sending cleaner water to the cistern is shown in the illustration. A more elaborate filter can be constructed by filling a tank or barrel with alternate layers of coarse gravel, charcoal and sand to cleanse the water before sending it to the house. All filters should be drained and cleaned when not in use.

If you want to use roof-collected water for washing up, brushing your teeth or drinking, first boil rainwater for 2 minutes or use Chlorine or Iodine treatment.

If your house doesn't have gutters, maybe it's time to think about adding them. An alternative is to construct a shed roof over a cistern tank at a high point of land and collect water there, then send it by gravity and pipe to your home. Use enameled steel for the shed roof, if possible.

Lentil Stew

1 Tablespoon olive oil
1 onion, chopped small
1 carrot, chopped small
1 stalk celery, optional
1 teaspoon salt
1 cup dried lentils, rinsed
4 cups water
1 teaspoon dried tarragon or thyme

Heat Dutch oven, add oil and onion, cook a few minutes. Add carrot, celery and salt, cook a few minutes, add lentils and water. Cover and cook about 30 minutes, stir in the tarragon or thyme. Taste and add a little salt and pepper if desired.

Mediterranean Vegetable Stew

6 servings

2 Tablespoons olive oil
1 large onion, chopped
4 cloves garlic, sliced thinly
2 cups cabbage, shredded
1 teaspoon salt
2 carrots, thinly sliced
2 potatoes, diced
1 large can tomatoes, chopped
2 teaspoons orange rind, finely minced
2 teaspoons fennel seed
1 quart stock
1 can red kidney beans or chick peas

Heat a Dutch oven or big pan, add oil and onion, cook a few minutes. Add garlic, cabbage and salt, cook 5 minutes more, stirring. Add remaining ingredients except for the beans, cover pan and let simmer until potatoes are tender. Stir in the beans. Heat.

Fill the Bathtub

Having a bathtub full of water is a great convenience for a bit of washing up. People who have sailboats claim they can do all the dishes for a crew in a teacup of water and you may have to do the same. Just scoop out a little at a time from the bathtub to wash your face but put a jar of fresh or **boiled** water near the bathroom sink for brushing teeth.

... And Cookbook

Other Possibilities

If a disaster catches you without a stored supply of clean water, you can use water in your hot-water tank, in your plumbing and in ice cubes. As a last resort, you can use water in the reservoir tank of your toilet (not the bowl), but purify it first.

A large picnic cooler may hold 20 to 30 gallons, as do large rubberized trash containers. If you keep a bag or two of ice in your freezer, put the bag into a clean, leakproof container so the water can be used when the ice has melted.

A 50-gallon water heater will have 50 gallons of drinking water even after the water heater has been turned off. Start the water flowing by turning off the water intake valve and turning on a hot-water faucet. If you drain your electric water heater, be sure to refill it before restarting when the power comes back on. If you forget, the heating element could easily be ruined.

Water beds hold up to 400 gallons, but some water beds contain toxic chemicals that are may not be fully removed by many purifiers. If you designate a water bed in your home as an emergency resource, drain it yearly and refill it with fresh water containing two ounces of bleach per 120 gallons. Use the water to clean, but don't drink it.

To use the water in your pipes, let air into the plumbing by turning on the highest (elevation) faucet in your house and draining the water from the lowest one.

Do you know the location of your incoming water valve? You'll need to shut if off to stop contaminated water from entering your home if you hear reports of broken water or sewage lines. Also, in cold climates frozen pipes may burst if there is no heat. Shut off the water and drain the pipes if there's a strong possibility of this occurring.

Care of Plants

To conserve water, place a plastic bag over house plants, fastening at the base with rubber bands or string. This will create a mini-greenhouse so plants will survive without frequent watering.

There is a time in the life of every problem when it is big enough to see, yet small enough to solve.

—Mike Leavitt

"I cannot be optimistic and I am generally concerned about the possibility of power shortages.... Supermarket supplies may be disrupted.... It's clear we can't solve the whole problem, so we have to allow some systems to die so mission-critical systems can work.... Pay attention to the things that are vulnerable in your life and make contingency plans.... Don't panic, but don't spend too much time sleeping, either."

Senator Robert Bennett
Chairman of the Senate's Special Committee
on the Year 2000 Problem

Step 3. Waste Disposal

If you have ever been invited to go sailing on a lovely sailboat that lacks a head (or *bathroom*, to landlubbers), you may have been advised that should the need arise, just "Bucket and chuck it." Down in the saloon, behind a curtain perhaps, will be a bucket. After use, one takes the bucket up on deck and after carefully judging which way the wind is blowing, one chucks the contents overboard into the sea. A simple, neat solution for disposing of waste at sea. A home owner with a bit of land can chuck it in the flower garden or hedge. What else can one do on land when power fails, water is shut off and one can no longer flush a toilet?

FIRST, remember that there's **one flush** in the tank when the power shuts off, and that valuable resource must not be wasted! Have a sign ready to hang on the toilet seat advising:

DO NOT FLUSH

Better tie a bow on the handle to get one's attention! You will appreciate the ability to flush that one tank after a few days of use. Hang out the sign Friday night, December 31st, just in case.

A camp toilet seat, placed over a sturdy pail or bucket, makes going to the bathroom comfortable for children and adults alike. If anyone in the family has had a hip or knee replacement, there may be an extended commode chair in the attic. The time may come to dust it off and place it over a heavy duty bucket.

Disposing of Wastes

An efficient way to dispose of sewage is to dig a trench in the back yard, about 1 foot deep and six inches wide, and have a pile of sawdust or mulch nearby. Dump the contents of the waste bucket in the trench and cover any solids with sawdust or mulch. An apartment dweller may want to designate a large trash can as waste receptacle for the duration, but it is better if the waste material can decompose aerobically (with air infiltration) than anaerobically (in closed containers or underwater). Anaerobic decomposition produces ammonium and other smelly gases. So sawdust or straw piles, turned regularly, are preferable to closed cans or boxes.

Organic material (kitchen scraps, wood ashes, paper, brush and leaves; anything that decomposes rapidly) should be placed into a compost pile and turned regularly to allow aerobic digestion. This material can then be used in your garden. Because of the potential for harm from human pathogens, sewage should NEVER be put into the compost pile or garden. Urine is sterile and can be put into the garden or disposed of on the ground. It is good for the garden because it contains nitrogen, a natural fertilizer.

Anything that doesn't easily decompose (wood, metal, wire, plastic) should be recycled or stored until it can be collected for recycling.

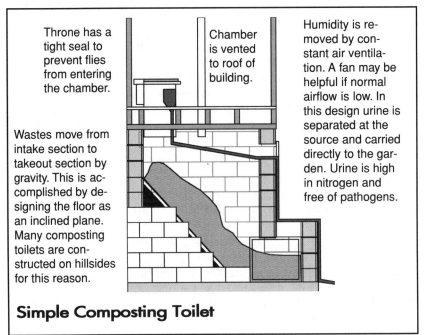

Throne has a tight seal to prevent flies from entering the chamber.

Chamber is vented to roof of building.

Humidity is removed by constant air ventilation. A fan may be helpful if normal airflow is low. In this design urine is separated at the source and carried directly to the garden. Urine is high in nitrogen and free of pathogens.

Wastes move from intake section to takeout section by gravity. This is accomplished by designing the floor as an inclined plane. Many composting toilets are constructed on hillsides for this reason.

Simple Composting Toilet

A simple flytrap can be added to any outhouse. Flies always take off by flying upward. By creating a box around the only upward exit, flies are trapped. Fly litter can be composted and used in the garden.

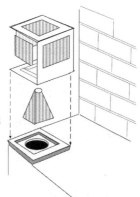

Dry Toilets

While water-based sewage disposal is considered normal in many Western countries, such systems are extremely expensive, costing about $4000 for each household to install and 25 to 60 gallons of water per person per day to operate. In many parts of the world, water is too scarce a resource to be used for sewage, and composting toilets have become the standard. A composting toilet can be safe, sanitary and efficient, if a homeowner is prepared to take the time required to properly manage the system. Many composting toilets are commercially available at costs ranging from $850 to $5000. In Australia there are even wet composting toilets whose flush water is recycled after biolytic digestion has occurred.

In an emergency, all you may have time to do is to build a pit latrine. But if you plan to be prepared for any emergency, or if you find yourself in an emergency that goes on for weeks or months, constructing a composting toilet is worth the effort.

Joe Jenkins' Design

Joe Jenkins' now famous *Humanure Handbook* describes the simple system his family has used on their farm for 20 years. It consists of a 5-gallon bucket that sits under a seat in the bathroom and gathers the solid (not the liquid) wastes. Emptied daily into a special compost pile, augmented with sawdust and other compostable materials, and turned weekly, Jenkin's system is odor-free and waste-free. After thermophilic digestion, the finished product goes to the orchard.

Clivus Multrum

The Clivus Multrum is probably the best known commercial composting toilet. Made of plastic or fiberglass, it is typically installed in the ground floor or basement of a house, with the pedestal being one or more floors above. Like all composting toilets, the Clivus works best if kept dry, either through a process of continual aeration, or through liquid separation at the source and discrete greywater disposal.

Dowmus

The Dowmus Company of Maleny, Australia offers a line of wet composting toilets that pass sewer water into a series of digestion chambers where specially adapted worms and bacteria break down the wastes into harmless soils. These wet digesters can not only accept shower and sink water, they can also compost kitchen scraps and paper trash. Newer models can be retro-fitted between floors of a two-story house.

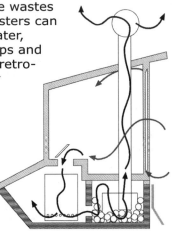

Sunny John

Created by John Cruickshank, the Sunny John is a simple set of plans to build your own composting toilet that creates a dry pile by evaporation. Air is drawn into the chamber by the thermal siphon effect created when a black painted stack is exposed to direct sunlight. The Sunny John is low-maintenance and inexpensive. Plans are available from John Cruickshank, 5569 N. County Rd. 29, Loveland CO 80538, hobbithouse@compuserve.com.

Solar Showers

Solar showers range form the simple black-plastic-bag variety found in sporting goods stores or the Campmor catalog to the more permanent stall design which can be constructed for about $300. Complete plans are available from Michael-Freeman, PO Box 220, Summertown TN 38483 (1-800-692-6329).

> *"...complex systemic problems...are inherently uncontrollable..., traditional approaches to solving them simply don't work.... They require collaboration, participation, openness and inclusion. These new systems' problems force us to dissolve our past practices of hierarchies, boundaries, secrecy and competition."*
> Margaret Wheatley and Myron Kellner-Rogers
> The Berkana Institute

"The Y2K bug provides us with an extraordinary opportunity to ask ourselves the profound questions which have been buried by our wealth and our technology. It is a time for us to ask what we really value and how we can preserve the ecological systems on which all life depends. It is a wonderful time to be alive."

—Robert Theobald, economist and futurist

Step 4. Heat and Light

In most Western countries we have become so accustomed to having electricity that we take it for granted most of the time. We use it to heat and light our houses, store and cook our food, wash and dry our clothes and dishes, heat our baths, and provide our home entertainment.

Many Canadians who experienced the ice storm of 1997 will never take electricity for granted again. Try doing without power for several weeks in the far North, in some of the worst weather conditions imaginable.

What would you do if electricity went out and stayed out for days? ...weeks?

1. Prepare Your House
Winterize your house, barn, shed or any other structure that may provide shelter for your family, neighbors, livestock or equipment. Install storm shutters, doors and windows; clear rain gutters; and repair roof leaks. Check the structural ability of the roof to sustain unusually heavy weight from the accumulation of snow or water, if drains on flat roofs do not work. Keep plywood, plastic sheeting, lumber, sandbags and hand tools on hand and accessible.

2. Dress Properly
If you go outside for any reason, dress for the season, and expected and changing conditions. If the weather changes, you don't want to be caught in the open with little protection. For cold weather, wear several layers of loose-fitting, lightweight, warm clothing rather than one layer of heavy

clothing. Outer garments should be tightly woven and water-repellent. Mittens are warmer than gloves. Wear a hat. Cover your mouth with a scarf to protect your lungs from extremely cold air. Wear sturdy, waterproof boots in snow or flooding conditions.

Heating with Wood

Heating most often involves burning a fuel. If you have a forested area near you from which you can cut firewood, you might consider a woodburning stove. New, top-of-the-line wood furnaces can cost several thousand dollars but are air-tight, burn combustion gases in a separate jacket, and have a catalytic converter on the exhaust port. They squeeze every available BTU from each piece of wood, meaning less work to keep the fire fed. Less elaborate models can be had either new or used for a few hundred dollars, but expect to burn more wood and get up in the night to keep it going.

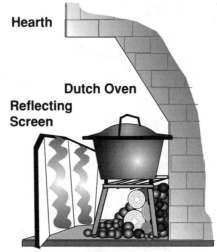

Hearth

Dutch Oven

Reflecting Screen

With a good wood furnace and an unlimited supply of wood, you can keep a whole house comfortably warm. With less wood available, you may want to go with a smaller woodstove and just heat one or two rooms.

Wood cookstoves, which were common 50 years ago, are harder to find now. New, airtight models which use coal, oil, or gas, hold a hot water reservoir, and have many other wonderful features, can cost more than $4000. More modest models, and good used cookstoves, can be found for less than $1,000. A good thing to remember about wood cookstoves is that while they are wonderful helping to heat the kitchen in the winter, all that heat is unwanted in the summer months, so alternative cooking methods (and summer kitchens) should also be considered.

There are commercially available wood-fired water heaters for $250 to $750. Some of these models also run on either wood or kerosene. A good catalog is *Alternative Energy Engineering,* in Redway, California. 1-800-777-6609, on the web at www.alt-energy.com.

I n the days when the wood range was king of the kitchen, grandma kept a woodbox next to the stove, filled with a selection of choices for every occasion: birch or sumac for a quick, hot fire with little body; maple and beech for longer-lasting, more dependable fires; oak and hickory for a slow, hot fire. An unsplit oak log was put into the fire just before bed and banked with ashes. Some coals would remain in the morning and keep the chill out of the kitchen.

Most cookstoves have four different dampers. The front damper is to the left and below the firebox. This is the primary draft channel to control the fire. Ashes drop through the grate into the ashpit below. Potatoes can be baked in the ashpit. The adjustable upper damper is called the "check." By closing the front damper and opening the check, you can cool the fire and save wood. The check is also how you regulate oven temperature during baking.

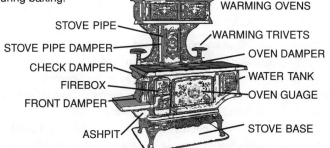

STOVE PIPE
STOVE PIPE DAMPER
CHECK DAMPER
FIREBOX
FRONT DAMPER
ASHPIT

WARMING OVENS
WARMING TRIVETS
OVEN DAMPER
WATER TANK
OVEN GUAGE
STOVE BASE

The stovepipe damper is the chief means of getting the fire going, and later, stopping it from burning too quickly and losing heat up the flue. The last damper is the oven damper, which is to either the left or right of the stovepipe at the back of the stove. When open, the heat goes directly to the flue. When closed, the heat circulates across the top and around the oven walls before going to the flue. An open oven damper spreads the heat evenly under the lid covers.

On a six-lidded cookstove, the hottest spot is between the left and center back lids. Opening the oven damper shifts the heat forward. A good cook shifts pots to find the appropriate temperature, and lets no-one else handle the dampers. The sides are for warming or simmering. The center is for a fast boil. To find out if the oven is hot enough for baking, you can use a stove thermometer, your hand, or thin scraps of paper, which will brown quickly if the oven is hot. Bread is best baked in a hot oven that is allowed to cool by shutting down the front damper and chimney damper, and cracking open the check. It may be necessary to turn the baking pans to assure evenness.

Old fashioned baked beans are prepared by leaving the covered iron pot in the oven all day, heated by a red oak log. Add water as needed, they will be ready by dinner. Soup can be kept on the stove top, with vegetables and more water being added through the course of the day.

If you burn wood:

1. Cure your wood for 6 months to a year after cutting. If you must burn wet wood, here is how to make the best of a bad situation: split the wood into small pieces about 3 inches in diameter; small pieces heat up and ignite faster, and burn cleaner. Try to let it warm up before burning burn small, bright fires, using no more than five sticks at a time.

2. If you have a battery-operated smoke detector, see that it is working; if you don't have one, try to get one. Get a stovetop thermometer from a local hearth store and keep track of the temperature. Burn creosote out of the chimney daily, when you first start the fire: you do this by creating a very hot fire (>500°F) listening as it roars through the pipe, and then cutting the draft and bringing the temperature down. This will prevent creosote buildup that can lead to a catastrophic chimney fire. Never leave a wood fire unattended.

3. Don't try to heat the whole house; concentrate all your activities in the room where the heater is and let the rest go cold. Drain down your water pipes where not heated. Shovel ashes into a metal container, take it outside immediately and empty it in the yard away from trees and shrubs. Never put a bucket full of ashes in the basement or on a wooden porch floor, and never put ashes in a wood or cardboard box. Keep small children away from the stove or fireplace, and fence off the ash pile.

3. Makeshift woodstove installations done by untrained people can be very hazardous. A proper masonry or metal chimney is needed. Check to see that the inside of the chimney flue is clear and smooth. Each joint in the flue pipes between a stove and its chimney must be secured with 3 sheet metal screws. Don't vent a wood stove out a window using single-wall pipe. Make sure there is plenty of space around the stove and flue pipe. Try to get professional help, even if it is just to get some advice by phone. Qualified people are listed in the yellow pages in categories like woodstoves, fireplaces, chimney sweeps.

4. Be careful using decorative fireplaces. If your fireplace doesn't make much heat, it is a decorative type and continuous use of it might be hazardous. If the unit has glass doors, it may be best to leave them open so you receive direct radiation from the fire. Close the damper until the fireplace starts to smoke, then open it until the smoking stops; this will reduce the amount of warm room air drawn up the chimney. Burn small, bright controlled fires; never overload the unit.

Please burn safely. Don't put your family at risk.

Chili

6 servings

1 large onion, chopped
2 Tablespoons oil
3 cloves garlic, minced
1 teaspoon salt
1 Tablespoon chile powder
1 Tablespoon cumin powder
1 teaspoon oregano
1/2 teaspoon allspice
1 15 oz. can tomatoes, chopped
1 15 oz. can black beans
1 15 oz. can red kidney beans

Heat a Dutch oven or large pan. Add oil and onions, fry 5 minutes, add garlic, salt and spices. Stir well, add tomatoes and beans. Simmer for 20 minutes. If you like it fiery hot, add a little cayenne pepper or crushed red pepper flakes.

Taco Salad

1 12 oz. bag corn chips
2 15 oz. can chili beans (or leftover chili)
1 onion, chopped fine
Lettuce or cabbage, shredded fine
6 oz. jar salsa

Warm the beans or chili, pour over corn chips. Top with the onion, shredded cabbage and salsa.

Lentil Curry

1 cup dried lentils
2 large onions, chopped
1 teaspoon salt
1 Tablespoon curry powder

Combine with cold water in a Dutch oven or large pan. Heat and stir. Simmer until lentils are soft, about 30 minutes.

Morocco Stew

1 large onion, chopped
1 Tablespoon olive oil
1 teaspoon salt
1 clove garlic, minced
1/2 teaspoon cinnamon
1/2 teaspoon coriander
1 15 oz. can garbanzo beans
1 15 oz. can tomatoes, chopped
1 15 oz. can sweet potatoes, diced
1/4 teaspoon crushed red pepper flakes

Heat a skillet, add oil and onion. Saute until tender, add salt, garlic, spices, beans, potatoes and tomatoes. Simmer for 10 to 20 minutes to blend flavors.

If you plan to cut your own firewood, be sure you have a large saw or chainsaw, and oil for the chain.

Borscht

6 to 8 servings

1 Tablespoon canola oil
1 onion, chopped
1 teaspoon salt
1/4 head cabbage, shredded
2 potatoes, peeled, diced
3 cups vegetable broth
1 15 oz. can diced beets, drained
1 teaspoon sugar or honey
1/4 cup ketchup

Heat a Dutch oven or soup kettle. Add oil, fry onion and salt 3 minutes. Add cabbage, carrot, potato and broth. Cover pan and cook until potato is tender. Stir in beets, sugar and ketchup. Heat to simmering.

Hot Sour Cabbage Soup

6 servings

1 Tablespoon olive oil
1/2 head cabbage, shredded
1 medium onion, chopped
1 large apple, peeled, chopped
5 cups vegetable broth
1 Tablespoon soy sauce
1 Tablespoon lemon juice
1 Tablespoon honey
1/4 teaspoon crushed red pepper flakes
1/4 teaspoon allspice

Heat a big pan, add olive oil, cabbage and onions and cook 5 minutes. Add remaining ingredients, cover pan, cook about 40 minutes until vegetables are tender. Chopped dried mushrooms are a good addition.

Curried Corn Soup

4 servings

2 Tablespoons chopped onion
1 Tablespoon canola oil
1 teaspoon curry powder
1/2 teaspoon salt
1 Tablespoon flour
3 cups milk or soymilk
1 16-oz can whole kernel corn

Heat pan, add oil and onion. Cook about 5 minutes, stirring occasionally. Stir in curry powder, add salt and flour. Slowly add milk, stir until mixture is smooth and slightly thickened. Add the corn, heat through.

Fireplaces

Now is the time to order a good supply of dry firewood for the winter of 2000 if you are fortunate enough to have one or more fireplaces in your house. A working fireplace can give you one warm room for cooking, eating and even sleeping (bring in mattresses from the children's beds or sleeping bags if the carpet is comfy.)

Most fireplaces are wood-burning, although coal can also be used to keep a fire going overnight. The best pots and pans for fireplace cookery are made of black cast iron. A good variety of cast iron cookware can be found in the Major Surplus catalog (800-444-8855). You can cook a variety of recipes with a black cast iron skillet and a Dutch oven that holds several quarts. Have a cast iron lid that will fit both pans. Cooking pans made of pyrex also work well in fireplaces. Have potholders or mitts handy.

Pans tipping over and spilling can be a problem with fireplace cookery, as logs burn down and break up, so pots need more watching than if you had put them in an oven. A useful accessory is a folding camp grill that will sit over the logs and coals and provide a level cooking area. Costs of these in the *Campmor* catalog (1-800-226-7667) range from $8 to $14.

Menu Ideas for Campfire, Grill, or Fireplace

Chili with Beans and Cornbread
Instant Rice with no-cook Peanut Sauce
Spaghetti Marinara and Garlic Flatbread
Taco Salad - Salsa - Chopped Onions
Barbecued Tofu - Baked Sweet Potatoes
Spicy Vegetable Stew and Couscous
Kasha with Bow Tie Pasta with Drop Biscuits
Curried Lentils with Rice and Chutney
Bean Burritos with Salsa
Tofu Links with Sauerkraut

Salad Ideas

Artichoke Hearts with Herb Dressing
Asparagus Tips with Herb Dressing

Dessert Ideas

Canned Fruit: Peaches, Pears, Pineapple, Apricots, Berries, Plums
Assorted Cookies, Rice Pudding, Applesauce, Vanilla, Chocolate or Butterscotch Pudding

---

If your fireplace is also your source of heat, and your house plan is fairly open, you may want to tack up blankets around the living/cooking area to keep that space toasty warm. You may want to set up a table near the fireplace, storing pans, utensils, dishes and tableware under it.

Outdoor Grills

Many people have a back-door barbecue pit or portable outdoor grill. Typically these are fueled by charcoal or propane, but in a pinch they could be converted to firewood. If you have a grill, make sure you have plenty of fuel stored. A large grill can supply the cooking needs of several families. Our favorite outdoor stove is the Rocky Mountain Volcano stove (www.rmvolcano.com). The Volcano is so efficient that

Grilled Flatbread (campfire, fireplace)

1 Tablespoon baking yeast
1 Tablespoon sugar
1 and 1/4 cups warm water, divided
4 to 5 cups flour (white or half whole wheat)
1 teaspoon salt
1/4 cup canola oil

Put yeast, sugar and warm but not hot water in a bowl. Let sit 5 minutes till bubbles form on surface. Add the cup of water, stir in the salt and oil and begin to add flour. Turn out on lightly floured surface and knead until smooth and elastic, about 10 minutes. Place in oiled bowl, turning to oil dough, cover and let rise until double (about 1 hour). Punch dough down and place in a loaf pan (for oven). Let rise again, 45 to 60 minutes.

After second rising, divide dough into 5 or 6 balls and roll one at a time to an even 1/8 inch thickness. Keep rounds on greased baking sheet. Brush tops with olive oil. To cook, place one round of dough on grill over burning coals, oiled side down. Brush top with oil. In 2 to 3 minutes, when grill marks appear on underside, turn bread over with tongs. Cook 2-3 minutes more until bread is cooked through. Keep warm. Flatbreads are good sprinkled with seeds and herbs just before baking.

Skillet Corn Bread   8 wedges

1 cup yellow corn meal
1 cup white flour
1/4 cup sugar
5 teaspoons baking powder
1/4 teaspoon salt
3 Tablespoons oil, divided
1 egg (optional)
1 cup milk or water

Heat the oven to 375° or have a good hot campfire going. Heat a heavy black skillet and add 1 Tablespoon oil to the hot pan. Mix cornmeal, flour, sugar, baking powder and salt. Stir in remaining oil and milk or water. Stir well and pour batter into the hot skillet. Place in oven or over coals and cook about 30 minutes. Stick a toothpick into center to check doneness.

12 to 20 charcoal briquettes are all that are needed to feed the whole family a full meal of rice, beans and cornbread.

In really difficult conditions, a portable outdoor grill can also be made from a metal wheelbarrow lined with aluminum foil and filled with charcoal, using the shelf from a gas or electric oven as a cooking rack.

Camp Stove

An assortment of stoves are available from camp equipment catalogs. For example, a small folding camp stove that uses solid alcohol fuel like Sterno is available for about $8. A more versatile two-burner propane camp stove costs about $50. A small bottle of gas will last 4.5 hours at low heat on one of these camp stoves. On high heat, you will run out of fuel in one hour.

A camp oven (about 11" x 11" x 11") can sit on top of a stove for baking and costs about $40. A four-slice folding camp toaster that can be placed over a burner is available for about $3.00.

Most camping supply stores have quite a wide variety of devices with which you can cook—from solar to Sterno.

Chafing Dish

At the turn of the last century, the chafing dish was the *fin-de-siecle* epitome of elegant entertaining. Delectable dishes from the chafing dish highlighted intimate candlelit suppers as both gentlemen and ladies prepared fondues, rich buttery sauces or blazing brandy-lit desserts right in the drawing room.

The chafing dish is heated by small cans of solid ethyl alcohol (brand name: Sterno). To prevent foods scorching, most use two pans: the bottom pan holds hot water, the top pan the recipe ingredients. Table top cooking could not be easier and one little can of fuel will burn for 45 minutes.

After the dish is served, the hot water in the bottom pan can be used to make tea or instant coffee or cocoa. Most one-dish meals lend themselves to chafing dish cookery.

Food Warmers

Food warmers, using short, round candles of votive size for fuel, are useful for keeping a sauce or small side dish warm.

Cooking with Gas

Gas cooking ranges are widely available in a variety of sizes and styles, but you should be aware that most of the newer models also need electricity. Some new gas ovens have "glow bars" that draw 300 to 400 watts. Others have spark ignition on the rangetop.

Turn off your electric main switch or unplug your gas range and see if you can still use your burners and oven.

Kerosene Heaters

Kerosene area heaters are found in most hardware stores. The advantage of kerosene is that it is easy to buy, easy to store, and easy to pour. It can also be used for lamps, camp stoves, and even some internal combustion engines. The disadvantages are that kerosene is dangerously flammable and some of us find the odor disagreeable.

Gas Heaters

Direct Vent Wall Furnaces mount on any outside wall and draw fresh air from outside and exhaust combustion by-products the same way. No electricity is required to ignite the pilot or operate the thermostat. They run on either liquid propane (LP) or natural gas. Costs range from $500 for 7,000 BTU to $650 for 33,000 BTU.

In subfreezing temperatures, a 200 sq.ft. room (20' x 10') takes 6000 BTUs/hr to heat. There are 92,000 BTUs per gallon of LP and 1,000 BTUs per cubic foot of natural gas. Therefore a small room will require 1 gallon of LP or 90 cu.ft. of natural gas every 15 hours to keep heated.

Heating a whole house may not be wise if fuel is limited. Room heaters, whether wood, kerosene, or gas may be a better choice than a furnace.

Even just heating a small room for 15 hours a day, a 5-gallon reusable gas bottle would last only 5 days. In these conditions, prepared-

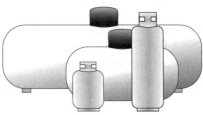

ness may mean having lots of warm clothes and blankets, **and** a full 250-gallon gas tank. If you are hooked up to the natural gas pipeline and your utility won't provide a tank for on-site storage, you might consider switching to LP gas and even having extra tanks installed.

Fire Safety

- If you use candles, place them in a safe place away from any flammable material.
- Be sure all children know the dangers of candles, chafing dishes, potpourri scent pots, the fireplace and space heaters.
- Never leave children alone near an open flame nor with matches.
- Keep clutter away from the stove while cooking.
- If grease catches fire, do not throw water on it. Cover the pan with a lid. Be careful. Moving the pan can cause the fire to spread. Never pour water on grease fires, nor try to beat it out with a towel.
- Always keep an A-B-C fire extinguisher close to hand.
- Do not store combustible materials in closed areas or near a heat source.
- Don't leave cooking food unattended for extended periods of time, since this is the most common cause of cooking-related fires.
- Only burn wood in the fireplace, and small amounts of paper at a time to avoid a chimney fire.
- Have your chimney cleaned and flue checked before using.
- Buy a battery operated smoke detector and a carbon monoxide detector. If you already have detectors, clean and test them. A working smoke detector can double your chances of survival.
- Practice home fire drills. Designate two exits from every room, make sure all family members are aware of an outside meeting place, and get out quickly.
- If your house catches fire, DO NOT ATTEMPT TO PUT IT OUT. Fire spreads faster than you can possibly imagine—a matter of seconds. Evacuate immediately. Contact the local fire department AFTER you have left the building. Even if you can't reach the fire department, do not try to put out the fire yourself.
- NEVER go back in to a burning building to retrieve belongings or pets.

Flash Water Heaters

Flash water heaters have been popular in Europe and the Far East for many years and can save you up to 50% of your energy costs compared to tank-type heaters. Flash heaters are "on-demand" type heaters that heat water only as it is needed, with no hot water storage. Two things about flash heaters need to be considered, however. One is that they all have a pilot light, which is a constant draw on your gas supply. The second is that they must be installed in a location that does not freeze. If the heat exchanger freezes, it will split and leak, rendering the flash heater useless.

If you are heating with an electric batch heater, typically a 50 gallon tank, you should seriously consider replacing it with a gas-powered batch heater or flash heater. Electricity is the most inefficient, and usually the most expensive, way to heat water.

Refrigerators

Most refrigerators are electric. Gas-powered models can be found, but they tend to be quite a bit more expensive. The Danby Gas Refrigerator and Freezer, made in Brazil, costs $1095. The Norcold LP, made in Sweden, costs $1265. A large gas refrigerator uses about 1550 BTU/hr, or one gallon of LP every 3 days.

Under average conditions, a standard electric refrigerator costs about $75 per year to power. A gas refrigerator takes about $150 per year. Because of this, many people are finding that it makes economic sense to switch to solar electric refrigerators like the SunFrost, which runs on either 12 or 24 volts. A SunFrost running without problems for 16 years is cheaper than a comparable electric, or 8 years for a comparable gas refrigerator.

Solar Power

It has often been said that our most reliable source of power is 93 million miles away and makes deliveries daily. Most of the world's energy—for growing food, building healthy bodies, and meeting our other basic needs—has always come from the sun.

To make solar power work for you, location is everything. You don't have to live at the Equator, you just have to point yourself in that direction.

Heating with sunlight involves capturing the long waves as they arrive from space and either putting them to immediate work or storing them for later use. Probably the simplest capture and storage device for the home is the greenhouse. Glass, plexiglass, clear fiberglass panels, or clear polyvinyl plastic sheets stretched over a frame of wood, metal conduit, or PVC pipe attached to the side of your house which faces the Equator will provide an instantly warm enclosure during most days of the year. Backing this space with

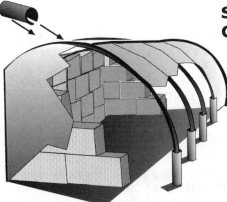

Strawbale Greenhouse

This simple greenhouse can be constructed with 36 bales of straw, one 20' x 20' sheet of clear polyvinyl, and five 12-foot sections of PVC pipe or steel conduit. To attach the clear poly, "clothespins" of PVC pipe (one size larger than the struts) are cut to 3-inch lengths and split up the middle. They snap on to the struts, over the poly cover.

strawbales, water drums, or any dark, solid mass (brick, stone, piled firewood) will provide storage of daytime heat, which will slowly be given back overnight.

Every house functions much the same as a greenhouse, except that direct sunlight only enters through windows on three sides and walls shade out most of the heating effect. Even if the fourth side has windows, the heating effect is nil, because those windows point away from the sun. At night, windows give off heat to the night sky. Therefore, to make any house into more of a greenhouse, it is important to un-cover all sun-side windows when the sun is on them, and to cover them again when the sun is not. The better insulating the cover, the more efficient will be the heat storage in the house.

The same principles apply to the basic solar box cooker, window box collector, flat plate and batch water heater, and most other solar heating devices. They point themselves at the sun, gather light through translucent windows, trap the light when it enters (typically by black or elm green coatings on walls or tanks) and then try to minimize heat losses with insulation.

Photovoltaic Systems

Using special crystals, solar electric cells produce electric-ity by converting incoming photon energy to the movement of current in a wire. Because these crystals are expensive to manufacture, solar electric power is not yet competitive with conventional sources for most applications, but scientific breakthroughs and an expanding scale of production are bringing prices down at a steady rate.

The size of a solar electric system depends on the amount of power that is required (kilowatts), the time it will be used (hours), and the amount of energy available from the sun (hours per day). You have control of the first two, your location controls the third.

A preliminary decision is whether your lights should be standard 110 volt AC or 12 volt DC. In a small home or RV, low voltage DC lighting makes sense and keeps the system costs down, because you don't need an inverter. Once you find you have the need for other appliances, or want to have more power than just the solar cells when it's not an emergency, an AC system is the choice. That means you may have to buy an inverter to convert battery power into normal house current.

Washing machines, large shop machinery, power tools and pumps require a large inverter, perhaps 2000 watts. A standard washing machine uses between 300 and 500 watt-hours per load. Vacuum cleaners use 600 to 1000 watts. Electric space heaters use 1000 to 2000 watts. Many small appliances like irons, toasters and hair dryers use even larger amounts, but because they require very short and infrequent periods of use, they can be managed. Stereos, televisions, VCRs and computers draw relatively small loads. Many of these are also available in 12 volt DC models that don't need an inverter.

Electric cooking, space heating, and water heating use a prohibitive amount of electricity for solar power systems. Going solar for lighting, radio and television, refrigeration, and some small appliances can make sense.

If you are considering going to a solar electric system, you should also look into other renewable sources of energy like windpower and hydropower. It is quite possible that, depending upon your location, these might provide a cheaper alternative to solar photovoltaic cells.

A typical American home consumes 10 to 20,000 kilowatt-hours (kwh) per year for all purposes. You can look at your electric bill to see what your home uses. Most parts of North America provide from 4 to 6 sun-hours per day, on average for the year. Let's say you can get by with 775 watt-hours/day (lights, refrigerator, fans, TV, radio) and you live in an area with 4 sun-hours per day (as most of North America):

Multiply the number of sun-hours by 50 Watts (panel rating) to see how many W/d each solar panel produces.

4 x 50 = 200 W/d

Divide that number into your load to see how many panels you will need.

775/200 = 4 panels

Multiply each panel's price by the number of panels.

4 * $500 = $2,000 total cost of panels

Multiply the daily load by number of cloudy days to have in battery storage.

$$775 * 7 = 5425 \text{ Wh}$$

Divide this by 12 to get Amp-hrs. Add 20% to prevent deep discharge.

$$3875/12 = 452 + 20\% = 542 \text{ Amp-hr}$$

Industrial chloride batteries start at about $1,350 for 525 Amp-hr.

System cost: $2,000 (panels) + $500 (mounting brackets) + $2,000 (inverter & controls) + $1,350 (batteries for one week storage, 25-yr life) + $1,000 (installation) = $6,850.

Unless you have very deep pockets, it should be evident from this analysis that with solar electric systems, a little conservation goes a long way. The use of energy-efficient appliances as well as nonelectric alternatives whenever possible can bring your load down dramatically. If you want to learn more about electric generating options we recommend *Home Power* magazine. A complete collection of back issues, which is available on CD-ROM at a very reasonable price, provides examples of installations using virtually every known source of power in any conceivable situation.

Lighting

Have some or all of the following on hand:

- Kerosene lamps + fuel and wicks: hurricane-style lamps are the most foolproof. Avoid the kind with thorium wicks (Coleman, Aladdin). They give off brighter light but produce radioactive soot.

- Flashlights + extra batteries: Consider especially the hand-crank flashlights in our resources section. Solar-recharged flashlights are notoriously unreliable, but a solar battery recharger is a good investment.

- Candles + candle holders: Go for the long-life candles and glass-enclosed candle lanterns.

- 12-volt auto bulbs, wire, and aluminum foil or tin reflectors. You can rig home lighting to run from a car battery, and use the car to recharge it.

"This is not a prediction, it is a certainty—there will be serious disruption in the world's financial services industry.... It's going to be ugly."
The Sunday Times, London

There are no shortcuts to any place worth going.
—Beverly Sills

"Failure to achieve compliance with the year 2000 will jeopardize our way of life on this planet for some time to come."

Arthur Gross
Chief Information Officer, IRS

Step 5.
Equipment and Tools

A major part of surviving a disaster of any type is being adequately equipped. There are tools and supplies that may help you get through an emergency. Some, like a water filter, candles and batteries, are for meeting the most urgent immediate needs. Others, like books on campcraft and gardening, are for longer term survival.

First, let's pack a short-term survival kit. This package is to be easy to carry around in a small backpack or in a car, to keep you alive for 3-5 days in any emergency. Within 3-5 days you should be able to either 1) Get help in a natural disaster situation, 2) Get to your main supplies, or 3) Be able to scrounge up something more substantial.

A company called Survival Inc. sells "72 hour kits" which contain food, shelter, and light for 72 hours (3 days), and would form a good basis for a home kit. (Survival Inc., 15600 S. Figueroa St. Gardena, CA 90248, 800-533-7415) Another good company is Nitro-Pak, which also deals in survival food and other supplies. (Nitro-Pak, 13243 E. Rosecrans Ave. Santa Fe Springs, CA 90670, 213-802-0099)

A survival kit should provide the following:

1. Food & Water - You should have at least 2000 calories of food, and one quart of water for a day. Single serving cans of chili, stew, beans, and soup are sold in supermarkets. Two 2-quart military canteens will provide a 4 day supply of water. Iodine tablets and a water filter are a good idea. These are available in most sporting goods stores.

2. Shelter - Also in sporting goods stores are a "space blanket" and a rain poncho. Both of these can provide overhead cover and warmth and are as small as a deck of cards when packed.
3. Heat and Light - A candle will not only provide light, but will also keep you warm when you bring it inside the space blanket with you. Matches are VERY IMPORTANT. Waterproof camping matches are best, although one can get book matches inexpensively and waterproof them by putting a coat of nail polish or wax on them. Cigarette lighters are useful. Other handy light sources are light sticks and Mini-Maglites.
5. First Aid - Start with the short list found in Step 1, but don't stop there. Add bandages, gauze pads, hemostats, scissors, blood pressure cuffs.
6. A Swiss Army Knife or a Leatherman Tool. You might also want to include some parachute cord, safety pins, sewing needles, and rubber bands. If you wear glasses, include a backup pair.
7. Communications - A whistle, air horn, or signalling mirror can draw attention if you are disabled. A battery-powered AM/FM, shortwave, or weather-band radio will keep you in touch with the outside world.

This is from the kit recommended by Chris Janowsky, who runs the World Survival Institute in Tok, Alaska, and is a regular contributor to the *American Survival Guide:*

Complete fishing kit
Gill net
Awl with extra thread
25 ft 550 cord
Carton cutter (razor knife)
Solar battery charger for AA rechargeable batteries
Signal mirror
Magnifying glass
2 pre-made wire snares
Bug dope (insect repellent)
Camo paint kit
Katadyne H2O purifier
Extra H2O purification tablets
Spool of nylon twine, holding safety pins and sewing needles
2 compasses (1 regular, 1 lensatic)
Duct tape
Waterproof notepad with pens and pencils
Space blanket
Thermometer
Altibaro (combination altimeter and barometer)
Spool of tripwire

Speed Pouch Inside Survival Kit:

Lock-back knife
EZ-Lap diamond knife sharpener
WSI Hot Spark flint
Fire starter
Small flashlight
Slingshot rubber
Surveyor's tape
Electrolytes

Medical Kit

6 3x3 gauze pads
4x4 gauze pads (6 doubles, 4 singles)
3 4x5 Kling bandages
3 3x5 Kling bandages
1 field dressing
10 Adaptic nonadhering dressings
Triangular bandage
Ace bandage
Assorted bandaids
Assorted rolls of tape, 1 waterproof
Safety pins, various sizes
Moleskin
Swab sticks
Field surgical instruments
Assorted sizes of suture thread and needles
Iodine
Antibiotic cream/ointment
Lanacaine cream
Eye drops
Tylenol
Bactine
Potassium iodine tablets
Ground yarrow flowers and leaves
Tums
Vitamins
Toothbrush
Dental powder
Dental floss
Snake bite kit (optional)

Fanny Pack

Fishing line, 2 kinds
Small crookneck flashlight
Mousetrap
Book: *Survival, A Manual That Could Save Your Life*
Waterproof collection bag
Net bag
2 ponchos
100 ft 550 cord
Sierra saw with extra blade
3 heavy-duty water bags
6 regular water bags

Chick Pea Patties

8 patties

2 15 oz. cans garbanzo beans, drained
1/4 cup flour
1 Tablespoon soy sauce
1 teaspoon onion powder
1/4 teaspoon garlic powder
1 teaspoon paprika
1 teaspoon dried parsley
1/2 teaspoon cumin powder

Mash beans, mash in flour and seasonings. Wet hands, shape into flat patties. Heat a skillet, add oil and fry patties until golden brown. Serve with hummus.

Misc Items for Belt

Canteen with drinking/cooking cup and outside pocket for water tablets, MagLight flashlight, Leatheman utility tool, large knife with sheath.

Essential Equipment for the Tool Shed or Closet

Now let's look at the longer term. Start acquiring:

Heat and Light
Firewood, fire starter
Large axe, maul, wedge, small
  hatchet
Bow saws and blades
Chainsaw, chains and bar oil
Gasoline, Sta-bil (stabilizer), oil
Candle lanterns, long-burning
  candles
Kerosene lights, fuel, wicks
Solar charger and Ni-Cad
  batteries (D, AA,AAA)
Blankets and sleeping bags
Warm clothing, hats, gloves
Workboots and woolen socks
Matches and lighters

Food Production and Storage
Chafing dish and fuel
Volcano stove and charcoal
Camp stove and butane tank(s)
Non-hybrid garden seeds
Seed starting trays
Black and clear polyethelene
Watering can and misters
Maximum-minimum recording
  thermometer
Grain/corn/cereal hand mill
Water-bath canner
Canning jars and lids (pint,
  quart, gallon)
5-gallon round buckets with
  rigid lids
Plastic bags, mesh bags,
  baskets and crates
Diatomaceous earth
Mylar bags and liners
Heat sealer for plastic bags
Oxygen absorbers

Water and Sanitation
Solar shower
Washtubs, washboard, deter-
  gent
Clothesline, clothes pins
Handcrank spout pump
Water filter pump and filters
Water purification tablets,
Water storage drums (black)
Non-electric washing machine

Chlorine bleach, calcium
  hypochlorite, hydrated lime
Toilet paper and paper towels
Sanitary napkins and tampons
Portable water containers
Pick and shovel
Narrow (well-gauge) water
  bucket—if you have a well

Miscellaneous
Shortwave radio
Binoculars, night scope
Bicycle patch kit, tubes, tires,
  pump
Diesel electric generator and
  extra gasoline
Shoelaces, extra shoes
Work gloves
Come-a-long
Sharpening tools, WD-40
Rope, nylon cord, and string
Bungee cords, duct tape
Rubber bands, paper clips,
  tacks
Bolts, screws, nails
Pencils, paper pads, notebooks
Extra eyeglasses
Board games, puzzles, domi-
  noes, crayons
How-to books
Other entertaining reading
Chisels, prybars and hand drills
Pliers, cutters and screwdrivers
Saws, shaping and cutting tools
Wrenches, ratchets, clamps
Drywall and masonry tools
Torches and solder
Welding tools and welding rod
Grease
Hand cleaner
Lumber and plywood
Strawbales
Wire mesh, several grades
Sleeping cots
12-volt car batteries, distilled
  water & electrolyte

Marinated Cannelini Beans

4 servings

1 can cannelini beans or small limas, drained
1 clove garlic, minced
1/4 cup olive oil
2 Tablespoons red wine vinegar
1 teaspoon dried parsley
1/2 teaspoon crushed oregano
1/2 teaspoon crushed basil
1/4 teaspoon dried tarragon
Salt and pepper to taste
Mix all together, cover the dish, let stand several hours to develop flavors.

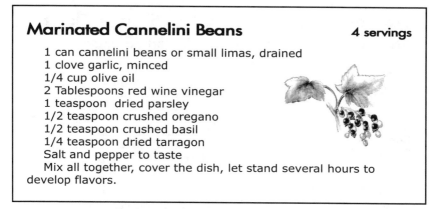

Catalog Shopping

There are many fine catalogs which provide essential tools and supplies for self-sufficiency and home preparedness and we can only list a few of the better ones. Most of these will accept credit card orders by phone and a few have on-line shopping. It is possible that by naming these suppliers, many of them will become overwhelmed by orders. You can find a regularly-updated list of suppliers of hard-to-find items at www.y2ksupply.com. Here are our current favorites:

Alternative Energy Engineering, PO Box 339, Redway CA 95560; 800-777-6609 (www.alt-energy.com), good prices and service.

Campmor, 810 Rt 17N, Paramus, NJ; 800-226-7667 (www.campmor.com, info@campmor.com), complete selection on campcraft.

Cumberland General Store, #1 Highway 68, Crossville TN 38555; 800-334-4640 (www.cumberlandgeneral.com). An old time store in the best sense.

Hard-to-Find Tools, 17 Riverside St, Nashua NH 03062; 800-926-7000 (www.brookstoneonline.com), as their name implies.

Jade Mountain, PO Box 4616, Boulder CO 80306; 303-449-6601 (www.jademountain.com), "appropriate technology" of all kinds.

Lehmann's Non-Electric Catalog, Box 41, Kidron, OH 44635; suppliers to the Amish for more than 45 years, wide range of woodstoves.

Major Surplus, 435 W. Alondra Blvd., Gardena CA 90248; 800-441-8855, best prices on dutch ovens and other ironware.

Radioland, 558 10th St, Fortuna CA 95540; 800-522-8863 (www.ccrane.com), imports the handcrank Bay-Gen radio. Lots of electric tools.

Real Goods Company, 555 Leslie St., Ukiah, CA 95482; 800-762-7325 (www.realgoods.com), the oldest and largest US supplier of renewable products for energy independence.

Rocky Grove Sun Co., HC 65, Box 280, Kingston AR 72742; 501-677-2871, have a $3 solar electric design guide.

"It's far too late, and things are far too bad, for pessimism."
Dee Hock, Founder, Visa International

*"A few months ago people were talking about seeing
the light at the end of the tunnel. Now the only hope is
keeping the world economy from total deterioration.
And you get a sense that it is all now truly left to Adam
Smith's invisible hand—it's beyond any country's
ability, and institution's ability to control."*

Jeffrey Garten, Dean, Yale School of Management

Step 6. Storing Food

Storing food without refrigeration is something humans learned to do more than 10,000 years ago, and most of our families have only forgotten in the past century.

If the electricity goes off...

FIRST, use perishable food and foods from the refrigerator.

THEN use the foods from the freezer. To minimize the number of times you open the freezer door, post a list of freezer contents on it. In a well-filled, well-insulated freezer, foods will usually still have ice crystals in their centers (meaning foods are safe to eat) for at least three days.

FINALLY, begin to use nonperishable foods and staples.

Principles of Good Storage

Storing food properly requires paying attention to several factors:

- Temperature
- Moisture
- Air circulation
- Light
- Insect Paths

Temperature is very important. Generally speaking, the warmer your storage location, the shorter the shelf life of the food being stored. A *recording thermometer* will not only show you the current temperature, it will track the highest and lowest temperature recorded in that location until you reset it. Place one in a potential storage area, record the temperature range after 24 hours and try another place.

Potential storage areas in your home include basement, attic, garage, closet shelves, or under beds and tables. Space under a deck or porch might work with some additional protection such as bales of straw and fencing to keep animals away.

For food being stored less than 2 years, the easiest and least expensive way to obtain it is to grow it or buy it from the grocery or farmers market. If food is to be stored longer than 2 years, it makes economic sense to buy from suppliers of long-term storable food (dehydrated and vacuum and gas packed). Start paying attention **now** to the shelf life of what you normally purchase and eat, dating packages, boxes or tins, rotating supplies to maintain freshness and keeping a record. How long does a 5 pound bag of flour last in your house? Sugar? A carton of oatmeal? A quart of canola oil? Make shopping lists, save them for a month, add up the quantities.

If canned food freezes...

Accidental freezing of canned foods will not cause spoilage unless jars become unsealed and contaminated. However, freezing and thawing may soften food. If jars must be stored where they may freeze, wrap them in newspapers, place them in heavy cartons, and cover with more newspapers and blankets. Freezing can break glass jars.

Planning What Foods to Store

1. Write a list of dishes frequently eaten, or a list of favorite meals.
   a. Create a list of typical meals. Post this list in a prominent place in your kitchen for the next 2 weeks. Each time you think of a new food write it on the list. Ask the family for suggestions. Make the list reflect what your family enjoys. Studies show families will eat the same 10 to 15 main food dishes 80% of the time.
   b. Create a separate list for breakfast and lunch foods, as appropriate and if desired.

2. Go back over the list and add foods needed to balance meals.
   After the main dish add foods to complete the menu: something from the bread group, the fruit group, the vegetable group, and so forth.

3. Inventory food you have on hand.
   a. Group foods according to category. For example, use one page for food in your freezer at present, one for what's on cupboard shelves, one for the root cellar, etc.
   b. List items and amounts of each. Update inventory on a regular basis.

4. Be a good shopper as you replace and add to inventory.
a. Watch for good buys, buy in bulk, use coupons. Gradually increase the amount of food stored.
b. Spend 40% of each food dollar on storage items, 60% will go toward fresh foods, special or seasonal foods.
c. Date all foods going into storage.
d. Place new foods at the back of the storage area. Use old foods first.
d. Add newly purchased food amounts to inventory list.

5. Store foods your family likes.
a. It is difficult to imagine much enthusiasm at the breakfast table if a family were to sit down to boiled wheat, with powdered milk and a vitamin pill. Additionally, a marked alteration in diet could cause some temporary digestive problems. If a family prefers corn flakes or raisin bran, milk, sugar, juice and toast for breakfast, these are the foods to store.
b. Take into consideration ages of the children and food allergies, if any.
c. Don't forget to include in your stored goods "comfort" foods like popcorn, cookies, hard candy, granola bars, and other snacks or desserts. In a time of disaster, food that tastes good or reminds you of better times can provide an important psychological boost.

6. Store Absolute Emergency Items, too.
Bulk quantities of wheat, corn, beans and salt are inexpensive and have nearly unlimited shelf life. If necessary, you could survive for years on small daily amounts of these staples.

Accumulate these items:

Wheat, rice, corn and dried beans
Powdered and evaporated milk
Iodized salt
Vitamin C and multivitamins
Grapefruit seed extract
Canned juices, milk, soup
Sugar and honey
Spices (pepper, garlic, onion, oregano, curry and chili powder)
Baking powder, baking soda, yeast
Olive oil and canola oil
Peanut butter and jelly
Dry, crisp crackers (in metal container)
Ready-to-eat canned foods
Baby food
Cereals, instant cereals, oatmeal
Potatoes (fresh and dried flakes)
Grits
Couscous, pasta (in a rigid container)
Foods for the elderly or those on special diets

Cheeses
Comfort/stress foods— cookies, hard candy, sweetened cereals, lollipops, instant coffee, tea bags, cocoa, canned nuts
High energy foods—granola bars, trail mix, chocolate bars
Soft drinks, drink mixes
Bouillion products
Vinegar
Aluminum foil
Utensils, cookware
Dishwashing liquid, bleach

> "Y2K is God's way of telling us we have to do this century over and over again until we get it right."
>
> —Mark Russell

Fireplace or Campfire Cajun Potatoes

Scrub potatoes, cut into chunks. Combine in a bowl oil and cajun seasonings (salt, pepper, chili powder, cumin, cayenne), roll potatoes in oil and place into foil packets. Fold foil and put packets on coals for 20 to 30 minutes, until potatoes are tender when pierced with a fork.

Roasting Chestnuts

With a sharp knife make a small slit on the flat side of each chestnut, piercing skin and shell. Oil the bottom of a cast iron skillet, add chestnuts, cover pan and place over medium low heat to roast. Stir from time to time or shake pan. After 20-25 minutes, test one for doneness. Both inner and outer skin should peel off easily. It will taste sweet and nutty, not starchy. Be careful not to burn chestnuts. Cool before cracking open.

Rice Noodle Pad Thai

(angel hair pasta can be substituted)

8 ounce package dry rice noodles
4 cups warm water
1 Tablespoon canola oil
3 cloves garlic, minced
1/2 cup shredded cabbage
1 carrot, peeled, grated
1 small onion, shredded
7 ounce can sliced water chestnuts
12 ounces tofu, diced small
1/4 cup soy sauce
3 Tablespoons rice vinegar
2 Tablespoons sugar
2 Tablespoons peanut butter
1 cup fresh bean sprouts (optional)
1 Tablespoon finely chopped peanuts

Pour 3 cups of warm water over the rice noodles and soak for 20 minutes. Drain and set aside, saving liquid for soup. Bring 1 cup of water to a boil and pour over the vegetables. Let stand 1 minutes, drain, save liquid. Heat a wok or large skillet, add oil, vegetables and drained noodles. Stir fry 1 minute, add tofu. Combine soy sauce, vinegar, sugar, peanut butter, stir into vegetable mixture, add sprouts. Cook 3 minutes. Serve garnished with the chopped peanuts.

Shelf Life

Generally speaking, the lower the temperature the longer the shelf-life. Persons storing foods in a garage at an average temperature of 90°F should expect a shelf-life less than half of what could be obtained at room temperature (60-70°F) which in turn is less than half the storage life in cold storage (40°F).

Keep a felt-tip marker with your food supplies. As you put groceries away, write the expiration date on the top of the package or can. Also note the date you bought the product, but remember, shelf life is based on the date of manufacture, not date of purchase. Sometimes you can decode the manufacture date from the packing code on the label. To learn more about packing codes and what they mean, visit www.idir.net/~medintz/surv_faq/asciifaq.txt. Here are some common items and their shelf lives, unopened, stored in a dry basement, below 70°:

Keeps for 3 to 5 years
Dried pasta (in a rigid container)
TVP

Keeps for 24 months:
Canned vegetables and fruits
White rice
Dehydrated potatoes (place boxes or bags in rigid containers)
Coffee in cans
Loose or instant tea (in a jar)
Sugar, artificial sweeteners
Vinegar
Baking soda
Bouillion cubes, granules

Keeps for 18 months:
Baking powder
Confectioner's sugar
Jams and jellies, mustard, ketchup, condiments
Molasses
Hot roll mix
Instant coffee, cocoa, tea bags

Keeps for 12 months:
Dried beans, peas, lentils
White flour
Dried fruits (air & moisture proof packages)
Honey
Nuts in airtight packages
Syrups (unopened)
Dried soup and instant pudding mixes
Grits, cornmeal
Condensed or evaporated milk (inverted at 2-month intervals)
Cold breakfast cereals (unopened)

Keeps for 6 to 12 months:
Fresh food in ventilated boxes in a moderately dry basement at 35 to 60°F.
Gravy and sauce mixes
Dried vegetables
Instant potatoes
Pancake mix
Crackers
Oatmeal
Biscuit, brownie and cake mixes
Rice mixes
Brown rice
Canned fruit juices
Salad oils
Salad dressings
Nonfat dried milk
Brown sugar
Hot oat and wheat breakfast cereals

Keeps for 2 months:
Cookies, packaged
Mayonnaise
Pretzels, potato chips and most snacks
Dry cheeses (in containers)
Potatoes, ventilated box
Carrots
Cabbage
Beets
Sweet potatoes
Winter squash
Onions in a net bag or individually wrapped
Apples, wrapped individually
Oranges, grapefruit, tangerines, lemons, limes

Find a cool, dark place to store food. This might be the basement, the garage, or a shed out back. Our grandparents always had a root cellar, and it made good sense. Under the ground the temperature evens out to a steady 55°F, which is pretty good for storing many kinds of food. Avoid spaces that are above 68°F, which might be space near an appliance that produces heat, or is high up in a room or in a building. Warm and humid climates shorten the shelf life of many items.

Many staples and canned goods have a long shelf life. Always buy the newest product or batch on the store shelf. Buy fresh looking packages and avoid dusty, rusty, or old looking packages. Never purchase dented or bulging cans.

Cereal, Rice and Pasta

Edible grains have been found in ancient tombs, but you may have encountered small insects in grains fairly recently purchased. One way to insure a longer shelf life is to freeze the grain as soon as purchased. Leaving it in the freezer for just one day will kill the tiny, invisible eggs of insects so they cannot hatch when the grain remains on the pantry shelf for a year or more.

In addition to rice, cornmeal and oatmeal, consider other grains to have on hand. Couscous, bulgur, kasha, millet and buckwheat groats will add variety to your menus and require little time or water to cook.

Couscous, Bulgur, Kasha and Buckwheat

Just pour a hot liquid (water, bouillion, fruit juice) over the tiny yellow grains and let stand for 15 minutes. Bulgur wheat needs to stand for about one hour after hot water is added. For kasha or buckwheat groats, cook in twice as much water for 15 minutes.

A can of popcorn in its original container will keep for 3 years in a dry basement; in a box or package, it keeps 3 months.

Whole wheat flour has a short shelf life ranging from a few weeks to a few months. White enriched flour in a rigid container will keep for 1 year in a dry basement.

Store dry goods in original containers of paper or plastic packed into rigid mice-proof containers. Store in a dry basement, away from heat and light.

One pound of dry matter provides about 1600 calories of energy. Because energy is the most critical item in a food storage program (it will prevent the baby from being hungry) it should be considered first. Dried beans, flour, wheat, rice, sugar, dried fruits or vegetables, pastas or dried skim milk all provide about 1600 calories per pound. While 1600 calories will not adequately meet the energy needs of a hard-working large man it will quiet hunger pangs for individual members of a family. One pound of dry matter per person per day serves as a basis for a food storage program.

It is possible to convert some forms of food with short shelf-life into other forms with longer shelf-life. Fruits and vegetables can be canned or dehydrated.

Dried Milk

Regular and instant nonfat dry milk are made from skim milk that has been dried by spraying into hot air. Instant milk is regular milk which has been further processed causing it to clump together which results in a product that is easier to reconstitute with water than is regular nonfat dry milk. They both have the same nutrient composition. Regular nonfat dry milk is more compact and will require less storage space. The most common type of dried milk to be found in grocery stores is instant nonfat dry milk. Dried whole milk will not store as well as nonfat dry milk.

Cocoa-Chocolate Milk Mix

1 cup cocoa
1/4 cup sugar
1/4 teaspoon salt
4 cups nonfat dry milk
Combine ingredients and store in a tightly covered container. To use: For every cup of cocoa or chocolate milk desired, use 1/4 cup mix and 1 cup water. Combine part of the water with mix to make a smooth paste. Add remaining water and blend well. Heat cocoa or chill for chocolate milk.

Spiced Milk   serves 6

2 cups nonfat dry milk
1/2 teaspoon cinnamon
1/4 teaspoon nutmeg
1 tablespoon sugar
1/4 teaspoon salt
1 1/2 quarts fluid milk or water
Combine dry ingredients. Add part of liquid to make a smooth paste. Blend in rest of liquid and stir until smooth.

White Sauce

2/3 cup nonfat dry milk
1/3 cup white flour
1 teaspoon salt
1/3 cup canola oil
2 cups cold water
Mix dried milk, flour and salt. Stir in oil. Heat and stir. As flour bubbles, slowly whisk in water. Cook until sauce thickens and bubbles. Use for creamed potatoes. Add chopped rehydrated shiitake mushrooms for mushroom gravy.

Vanilla Pudding Mix

1 1/2 cups sugar
2 1/2 cups nonfat dry milk
1 1/4 cups flour
1 teaspoon salt
Stir the ingredients together until well mixed. Store in a tightly covered container in a cool place. Makes enough mix for 24 servings. Mix with twice as much water and cook until thickened.

Chocolate Pudding Mix

Add 1/4 cup cocoa and 1/2 cup more sugar to above ingredients before stirring.

Butterscotch Pudding Mix

Substitute 1 1/2 cups packed brown sugar for granulated sugar. To make pudding:
1 1/4 cups pudding mix
2 1/2 cups warm water
1 1/4 teaspoon vanilla
1 tablespoon margarine or butter
Combine mix with water in top of double boiler. Place over boiling water and cook until thickened, stirring constantly. Cover and cook 5 minutes longer. Add the butter or margarine. Cook over hot water for 1 minute. Stir in vanilla and chill. Serves six.

Whipped Topping

1/2 cup ice cold water
1/2 cup sugar
1/2 cup nonfat dry milk
2 tablespoons lemon juice
Put water into an ice cold bowl. Add dry milk and beat with a cold egg beater until stiff. Add sugar slowly while beating. Add lemon juice and beat only until well mixed.

In any recipe calling for milk, simply add the dry milk to other dry ingredients. Sift to blend, then substitute water for the milk called for in the recipe.

Whipped Topping No. 2

6 tablespoons nonfat dry milk
1 cup water
2 teaspoons gelatin
1 1/2 tablespoons cold water
1/4 cup sugar
1 teaspoon vanilla

Dissolve the milk in the cup of water and scald. Soak the gelatin in cold water. Combine the scalded milk, dissolved gelatin and sugar. Stir and chill until it jells. Now beat the mixture until it acquires the consistency of whipped cream. Add the vanilla and whip again.

Things to consider when buying dried milk:

1. It is best to buy dry milk fortified with vitamins A and D.

2. A claim of "No Preservatives" may be on the label to reassure customers; however, added preservatives are not legal therefore no dried milk processed in the U.S. will contain preservatives.

3. The label may say Grade A to indicate the quality of the milk used in the drying process. Essentially all processing plants producing dried milk use Grade A milk today.

4. "Extra Grade" on the label indicates that the processing plant has met certain criteria and the milk is slightly lower in butterfat and moisture content, more soluble, contains fewer bacteria, and contains fewer scorched particles.

5. The size of the container holding the dried milk should fit family need. Once a container is opened, the milk will not keep long, therefore, a very large container is not desirable for a household that consumes a small amount of milk per week.

6. Type of package becomes important if the dried milk is to be stored for long periods of time. The package should be water-proof and impermeable to air. Plastic films are good protection against oxygen over short periods of time, but metal cans should be used if dried milk is to be stored for more than a year. Storage times will be shorter for products stored in a warm place: 50°F 48 months; 70°F 24 months; 90°F 3 months.

8. Date the milk when you buy it. It is much more desirable to rotate your supply of dried milk by using the oldest first than to have milk with off-flavors. However, if you do have milk which has been stored too long and has developed some off-flavor, use it to make a potato-onion soup, or a quick bread containing dried fruit, like banana bran muffins. You can also use it in mashed potatoes with sauteed garlic or in a chocolate cake. Don't use it to make yogurt, pudding or a white sauce.

FOOD PLANNING FOR 6 WEEKS OF STORAGE

Product	Number of times served	Serving size	One person	Four persons
Fruit, tomatoes	7/wk	1 c.	10 q.	40 q.
Broccoli, spinach, carrots, squash	4/wk	1/2 c.	3 q.	12 q.
Asparagus, peas, cabbage, green beans, corn	7/wk	1/2 c.	5 q.	20 q.

The Home Storage Area

The storage area should be located where the average temperature can be kept above 32°F and below 68°F. Remember that the cooler the storage area the longer the retention of quality and nutrients. Freezing of some items, such as canned products, should be avoided since the expansion of the food during freezing may rupture metal or break glass, or break the seal and allow the food to be contaminated. This could pose a serious safety risk when the food thaws.

The storage area should be dry (less than 15 percent humidity), and adequately ventilated to prevent condensation of moisture on packaging material. The area should be large enough so that shelves can accommodate all of the stored food and adequate space is available to keep the area clean. A 9 x 12 foot room with 10 foot ceilings will provide adequate space for a family of six to store an 18 month supply of food. Food should not be stored on the floor. It is a good idea to have the lowest shelf 2-3 feet off the floor in flood prone areas. Shelves should be designed so that a simple rotation system can effectively allow the oldest food to be used first and the newest food to be held within the shelf-life period.

When designing and building a food storage area, do it to minimize areas where insects and rodents can hide. Seal all cracks and crevices with steel wool. Eliminate any openings which insects or rodents may use to gain entrance to the storage area. Heat producing electrical equipment such as freezer, furnace and hot water heater should not be housed in the storage area.

Containers

Food should only be stored in food-grade containers. A food-grade container is one that will not transfer non-food chemicals into the food and contains no chemicals which would be hazardous to human health. Some good examples of containers not approved for food use are trash or garbage bags, industrial plastics and fiber barrels that have been used for non-food purposes. There is no stored food that is worth enough to risk chemical contamination by non-food chemicals and a potential hazard to human health. Plastic films and containers of food-grade quality are made from polycarbonate, polyethylene and polyester. They differ in characteristics of density, strength and barrier properties. To increase moisture and oxygen barrier properties, films have been laminated. Laminated plastics may include a metallic layer which will greatly increase barrier properties. Military food packaged in metallized polyester, polyethylene wrap has a long shelf life (5+ years) if kept cool.

When safe packaging material has been identified, some suggestions as to size and durability are warranted. Containers for storage of dry foods such as wheat, beans, rice, oatmeal, and cornmeal should have a maximum of 20-25 pound capacity. These sizes may be moved easily by one adult. More important is that these smaller amounts of food will be used up in a relatively short period of time, thus reducing the chance for contamination or infestation by insects. Smaller containers provide a way of using the food, but not exposing large quantities to the environment during use periods. Metal cans used in the canning industry are designed to last a few years. Losses of canned foods usually occur due to breakdown of the can rather than extensive deterioration of the food under normal storage conditions.

Sealed number 10 cans are popular for dehydrated foods mainly due to size, convenience and minimal exposure of the foods to the environment. Glass jars, which are popular among home canners, are quite inert compared to metal cans, but are less shock resistant. Fiber boxes, which were the original containers for glass jars, make excellent storage containers for jars of fruit since they exclude light and effectively separate individual jars to prevent breakage. Glass, metal and plastic containers, especially if they have tight-fitting lids and no open crevices or seams, are usually the containers of choice. Glass jars have the advantage that you can see what's in them.

Flexible plastic containers last longer and are more durable if placed inside a rigid container. Information on the suitability of flexible plastic containers for protecting food from insect infestations is limited. If the food is insect-free to begin with, and if the packages are properly sealed, they should prove satisfactory.

One trick you can try to increase the shelf life of dry foods in packages is to freeze them when you bring them home from the grocery store. Make space in your freezer to store on a temporary basis rice, flours, dried milk, cereals, etc. 24 to 48 hours of being frozen will kill any eggs of insects that were left in the product when packaged by the manufacturer. This will greatly increase pantry shelf life. Keep rotating new purchases into the freezer space reserved for packaged foods.

Do not store non-food household chemicals in the same area with food. Volatile chemical compounds can be transferred to the food and affect the flavor and odor. These chemicals should be stored in a separate area where children do not have access to them.

Good housekeeping helps prevent insect infestations. To prevent or at least minimize insect infestations in stored food products it would be ideal to store them somewhere between 35°F and 45°F. Realistically, if they can be stored below 65°F it will be helpful.

Fumigation with Dry Ice Prior to Storage

To fumigate home stored wheat or similar products, spread about 2 ounces of crushed dry ice on 3 or 4 inches of grain in the bottom of the container, then add the remaining grain to the can until it is at the desired depth. If fumigating large quantities use 14 ounces for 100 pounds of grain or 1 pound of dry ice for each 30 gallons of stored grain. At approximately 75 cents a pound for dry ice the cost of fumigating is reasonable.

Since the fumes from vaporizing dry ice are heavier than air, they should readily replace the existing air in the container. Allow sufficient time (about 30 minutes) for the dry ice to evaporate (vaporize) before placing the lid on all the way. The lid should not be made tight until the dry ice has pretty well vaporized and has replaced the regular air. Then it can be placed firmly on the container and sealed. Should pressure cause bulging of the can after the lid has been put in place, remove the lid cautiously for a few minutes and then replace it. If using plastic bags in the can, don't seal the bags until the dry ice has vaporized. Carbon dioxide will stay in the container for some time, provided the container lid is tight. When practical, follow the above procedure in a dry atmosphere to reduce the condensation of moisture in the bottom of the can.

Dry ice tends to control most adult and larval insects

present, but probably will not destroy all the eggs or pupae. If a tight fitting lid is placed firmly on the container after the dry ice has vaporized, it may keep enough carbon dioxide inside to destroy some of the eggs and pupae. After 2 to 3 weeks another fumigation with dry ice may be desirable to destroy adult insects which have matured from the surviving eggs and pupae. If properly done, these two treatments should suffice. Yearly treatments are not indicated unless an infestation is recognized.

Basic Biscuits (for oven)

16 biscuits

2 cups white flour (or half whole wheat)
3 teaspoons baking powder
1/2 teaspoon salt
1/3 cup oil
1/2 cup milk or water

Stir dry ingredients together, add oil and milk, mix well. Turn out on a lightly floured board, knead 5 times, pat down to 1/2 inch thick. Cut rounds with 2 inch biscuit cutter or glass. (Or cut squares with knife). Put on baking sheet and bake in a hot oven (375°) 25 to 30 minutes.

Variations:

Add to dough 1/2 cup grated cheese or 1/4 cup good tasting nutritional yeast for **cheese biscuits**.

Add to dough 1 Tablespoon sugar and 1/2 cup dried fruit (raisins, currants, blueberries, cherries) for **fruit biscuits**.

Drop Biscuits (stovetop, oven, campfire)

Use the same ingredients as above, but add 2 Tablespoons more milk or water and drop dough onto oiled pan surface. Place pan on coals or stovetop, cover pan, cook until done. Variation: Add cheese or nutritional yeast or dried fruits as above.

Flour Tortilla

4 tortillas

1 cup flour (white or half whole wheat)
1/2 teaspoon baking powder
1/4 teaspoon salt
about 1/3 cup warm water

Mix dry ingredients, stir in enough water to make a dough that holds together. Knead a few times, divide into 4 balls. Cover with a towel to rest 15 minutes. Flatten into 8-inch rounds, using tortilla press, rolling pin or your hands. Cook on an ungreased hot pan or griddle. Turn as soon as blisters form, about 30 seconds. Cover cooked ones with a towel to stay warm.

Small quantities of grain, 1 to 10 pounds, can be put in medium to heavy food grade plastic bags and placed in a deep freeze for 2 to 3 days. This will usually destroy all stages of any insect pests which are present. As a check spread the deep freeze treated grain on a cookie tray at room temperature until thawed. If live insects are present they will probably be seen crawling about. If they are present, repeat the process. If not, remove any insect fragments, put the grain in an approved container and store it in a cool, dry place.

Root Cellars

The main reason for having a root cellar is to keep vegetables from freezing in the winter. The temperature of the earth 10 feet below the surface stays at a constant 55 degrees. Because of the movement of air, root cellar temperatures usually stay between 50 and 70, which is optimal for storing many vegetables. Because they are constructed underground, most root cellars will be damp with condensation. For this reason, they may not store some crops, like grains, onions, garlic and fruit, as well as they store potatoes, squash, cabbages and carrots.

You should do what you can to prevent heat from having access to your cellar. This includes:

- Having your root cellar in the shade throughout the day
- Wise use of insulation
- An access hatch that opens to the top (hot air rises, cold air falls)
- Building on the north side of hills
- Building in the basement of your home

Having a second door on one side is a good idea if you don't want to have to search for the hatch door when it is under 3 feet of snow.

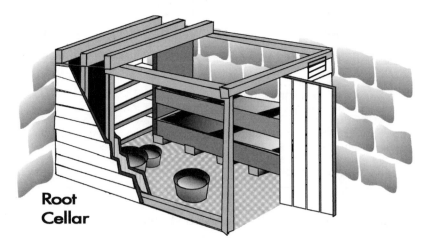

Root Cellar

Basic Yeast Bread

1 Tablespoon baking yeast
1 Tablespoon sugar
1 and 1/4 cups warm water, divided
4 to 5 cups flour (white or half whole wheat)
1 teaspoon salt
1/4 cup canola oil

Put yeast, sugar and warm but not hot water in a bowl. Let sit 5 minutes till bubbles form on surface. Add water, stir in salt and oil and begin to add flour. Turn out on lightly floured surface and knead until smooth and elastic, about 10 minutes. Place in oiled bowl, turning to oil dough, cover and let rise until double (about 1 hour). Punch dough down and place in a loaf pan (for oven). Let rise again, 45 to 60 minutes. Bake at 375° for 15 minutes, reduce heat to 350° and bake about 40 minutes more. Tip out of pan to cool.

Rolls conserve heat, because they bake in about 18 minutes. After initial rising, shape dough into 16 to 18 round rolls or breadsticks. Let rise again, bake. For variation, add seeds like caraway, fennel, flax, sesame or poppy seeds to dough. Or make herb rolls by adding 1 Tablespoon dried dill weed or basil or oregano to dough or a combination while kneading.

Unhurried Whole Wheat and Oatmeal

4 cups fresh ground flour
1/2 cup rolled oats
1 1/2 cup liquid (milk, yogurt, water)
1 teaspoon yeast
1 teaspoon salt
2 Tablespoons sweetener (sugar, honey, molasses, sorghum)
2 Tablespoons oil

Heat liquid to 105°F, pour into large bowl and add sweetener. Stir in yeast and allow to stand. Stir in flour and oats until mildly thick. Allow to stand for 3 hours. Add salt and oil and begin to work dough, adding more flour. It should not stick to the bowl. Allow to rise for 1 hour, then knead on a lightly-floured surface. Do not add too much new flour at this stage. When only slightly sticky divide into well-oiled pans and let rise 30 minutes. Place in oven preheated to 350°, bake 35 minutes and test by tapping the bottom for hollow sound.

Cinnamon Raisin Bread

After bread has risen, roll it out into a rectangle. Spread with butter or margarine, sprinkle with 1/4 cup brown sugar and 1/2 cup raisins. Roll up tightly and put in loaf pan to rise.

You can borrow cool from the air. Often the night's air temperature will be cooler than the air in your cellar. During the spring and fall of the year, open your vents (and even perhaps the door) at night when the temperature is dropping below the temperature of the air in your cellar. Close them early in the morning before the outside air warms up. (Don't do this if the temperature is expected to drop below freezing.)

Another important consideration is humidity. In a dry environment, your vegetables will soften and shrivel up. Underground root cellars will generally maintain humidity if they have an earth or dirt floor.

The best root cellars have vents. This is because the vegetables in your cellar give off gases that are conducive to either spoilage or sprouting. For example, apples naturally give off ethylene gas which makes potatoes sprout prematurely.

Good venting fundamentals include:

- Have an inlet vent and an outlet vent.
- The outlet must always be at the highest level in the cellar with the outlet tube flush with the inner wall.
- The inlet should come into the cellar at the bottom. This is easily done if your cellar is built into a hill, but nearly as easy if it is buried in flat ground. With your inlet vent opening on top of the ground near your outlet vent, your inlet vent pipe must go all the way to the floor before opening into your cellar.
- Keep shelves a couple of inches away from the walls of the cellar. This will greatly promote circulation around the vegetables stored on these shelves. Use rot resistant or pressure-treated wood.
- To prevent your potatoes from sprouting prematurely, keep your apples above them so the circulating air moves away from your potatoes.
- Have a system in place to close your vents in freezing weather. Something as simple as a big sponge can work for this. If you have very cold winters, you may wish to block off both ends of each vent pipe.

What Size Cellar?

A 5 foot by 8 foot root cellar will store 30 bushels of produce. An 8 foot by 8 foot cellar should hold plenty for the average family. A 10 foot by 10 foot cellar should take care of everything you can produce.

Your cellar should be graded so any water will run or seep out the door. In a very damp or very dry area you will want to put down three inches of gravel. If your cellar is unusually wet, you may want to dig a sump in the middle of your cellar floor and fill this with gravel, along with the three inches on the floor.

You may wish to build two rooms in your cellar, one with a cement floor for lower humidity storage items, and another room with earth floor or a wide-gapped wood floor for higher humidity storage items. If you do this, the wall between the rooms should be as air tight as you can make it. If you have a venting system, you should have a separate set of vents for each room. The high-humidity storage area should be the far room in the cellar.

Keep a thermometer and humidity gauge in your cellar.

Keep the door(s) closed to your cellar as much as possible when it is warm outside.

If the humidity in your cellar is too low you can raise it by:

- Leaving at least the floor of your cellar exposed to the earth (a dirt floor or air gaps in your floor down to the earth).
- Sprinkling water on a gravel floor or laying out damp towels or burlap bags.
- Packing root vegetables in damp sawdust, sand or moss.

If you get much of a temperature fluctuation in your cellar, humid air as it cools past its dew point will condense on the ceiling, walls, and produce. Excess water on your goods can induce spoilage. Cover vegetables with burlap, towels, etc. to absorb excess condensing moisture. Also, if the air is condensing inside, open your vents if the air outside is cooler than it is inside. Even if it is very humid air, as it warms in the root cellar, its relative humidity will drop. Of course, the opposite can happen. If you let warm damp air in, moisture will condense out as it cools.

During extremely cold weather, if your cellar is threatening to freeze, put a light bulb inside. If you do this, you need to cover your potatoes so they won't turn green. (Do not use a kerosene lantern. Kerosene lanterns produce ethylene, which is a fruit ripener.) Also remember that snow is an excellent insulator. Don't tramp down or remove the snow on top of your root cellar any more than you have to in order to gain entry.

Principles of Home Canning

Home grown vegetables can be canned in season to enjoy in winter. Canning can be a safe and economical way to preserve food. Canning homegrown food may save you half the cost of buying commercially canned food, if you discount your labor costs. Canning favorite and special products to be enjoyed by family and friends is a fulfilling experience and a source of pride for many people. Companies that produce jars and lids for canning have excellent instruction booklets available.

If vegetables are handled properly and canned promptly after harvest, they can be more nutritious than fresh produce sold in local stores. The advantages of home canning are lost when you start with poor quality fresh foods; when jars fail to seal properly; when food spoils; and when flavors, texture, color, and nutrients deteriorate during prolonged storage. Store the jars in a relatively cool, dark place, preferably between 50 and 70°F. Can no more food than you will use within a year.

Advantages of Hot-packing

Hot-packing is the practice of heating freshly prepared food to boiling, simmering it 2 to 5 minutes, and promptly filling jars loosely with the boiled food. Whether food has been hot-packed or raw-packed, the juice, syrup, or water to be added to the foods should also be heated to boiling before adding it to the jars. This practice helps to remove air from food tissues, shrinks food, helps keep the food from floating in the jars, increases vacuum in sealed jars, and improves shelf life. Preshrinking food permits filling more food into each jar.

Hot-packing is the best way to remove air and is the preferred pack style for foods processed in a boiling-water canner. At first, the color of hot-packed foods may appear no better than that of raw-packed foods, but within a short storage period, both color and flavor of hot-packed foods will be superior.

Using Pressure Canners

Follow these steps for successful pressure canning:

1. Put 2 to 3 inches of hot water in the canner. Place filled jars on the rack, using a jar lifter. Fasten canner lid securely.
2. Leave weight off vent port or open petcock. Heat at the highest setting until steam flows from the petcock or vent port.
3. Maintain high heat setting, exhaust steam 10 minutes, and then place weight on vent port or close petcock. The canner will pressurize during the next 3 to 5 minutes.
4. Start timing the process when the pressure reading on the dial gauge indicates that the recommended pressure has been reached, or when the weighted gauge begins to jiggle or rock.
5. Regulate heat under the canner to maintain a steady pressure at or slightly above the correct gauge pressure. Quick and large pressure variations during processing may cause unnecessary liquid losses from jars. Weighted gauges on Mirro canners should jiggle about 2 or 3 times per minute. On Presto canners, they should rock slowly throughout the process.
6. When the timed process is completed, turn off the heat, remove the canner from heat if possible, and let the canner depressurize. Do not force-cool the canner. Forced cooling may result in food spoilage.

Cooling the canner with cold running water or opening the vent port before the canner is fully depressurized will cause loss of liquid from jars and seal failures. Force-cooling may also warp the canner lid of older model canners, causing steam leaks. Depressurization of older models should be timed. Standard-size heavy-walled canners require about 30 minutes when loaded with pints and 45 minutes with quarts. Newer, thin-walled canners cool more rapidly and are equipped with vent locks. These canners are depressurized when their vent lock piston drops to a normal position.

7. After the canner is depressurized, remove the weight from the vent port or open the petcock. Wait 2 minutes, unfasten the lid, and remove it carefully. Lift the lid away from you so that the steam does not burn your face.
8. Remove jars with a lifter, and place on towel or cooling rack.

Storing Canned Foods

If lids are tightly vacuum sealed on cooled jars, remove screw bands, wash the lid and jar to remove food residue; then rinse and dry jars. Label and date the jars and store them in a clean, cool, dark, dry place. Do not store jars above 95°F or near hot pipes, a range, a furnace, in an uninsulated attic, or in direct sunlight. Under these conditions, food will lose quality in a few weeks or months and may spoil. Dampness may corrode metal lids, break seals, and allow contamination and spoilage.

Sauerkraut

Two hundred years before Vitamin C was ever heard of, sauerkraut was used for curing scurvy and rickets. Sauerkraut is both a European and Asian favorite winter food because of its health-giving properties and longevity.

To make sauerkraut you will need one pound (2 cups) of salt for 40 to 50 pounds of cabbage. Approximately 45 pounds of cabbage will fill a 5-gallon crock. Shred cabbage to about the thickness of a dime. Mix 5 pounds of shredded cabbage to 1/4 cup salt thoroughly and let stand 5 minutes. Pack in clean container by hand and press to draw the juice, continuing for as many batches as it takes to fill container. Cover the cabbage with clean cloth (several layers) and tuck it down the sides. Close the container with a lid that rests inside, covered with a weight of such size that the juice comes to the bottom of the lid but not over it. The weight may have to be varied over the first few days of fermentation. Keep at 68 to 85°F for 2 to 6 weeks. The warmer the temperature, the faster the fermentation.

Remove white scum forming at the brine surface promptly or it will use up the acid and spoil the kraut. Lift the cloth carefully so that the scum adheres, rinse the cloth and lid, and replace. You will need to do this every day or two. If brine becomes too low, you can add additional brine using 2 tablespoons of salt to one quart of water.

Once the sauerkraut has matured (light color, not pink, no rotting smell) you can sterilize and preserve it by the hot-pack canning method.

Butters, Jams, Jellies, and Marmalades

Sweet spreads are a class of foods with many textures, flavors, and colors. They all consist of fruits preserved mostly by means of sugar and they are thickened or jellied to some extent. Fruit jelly is a semisolid mixture of fruit juice and sugar that is clear and firm enough to hold its shape. Other spreads are made from crushed or ground fruit.

Chutney

2 pounds apples, peeled, cut in 1-inch chunks
1 lemon, thinly sliced, slices quartered
1 1/2 cups sugar
3/4 cup cider vinegar
1/2 cup chopped onions
1/2 cup raisins
2 Tablespoons gingerroot, minced
1 teaspoon salt
1 teaspoon black mustard seed
1/2 teaspoon cardamom
1/2 teaspoon red chile pepper flakes

Combine all ingredients except fruit and bring to a boil in a large kettle. Add fruit, cover pan, cook, stirring occasionally, until fruit is tender but firm when pierced with a fork. Ladle into hot sterile jars and seal. Peaches, pears or mangoes can be used.

Bombay Chutney

1 onion, finely chopped
1 potato, diced
1/2 teaspoon cumin seeds
1/2 teaspoon tumeric
1/4 teaspoon mustard seeds
1/2 teaspoon tamarind paste
2 green chillies
3 Tablespoons whole wheat flour
Salt to taste
1 1/2 Tablespoons cooking oil

Warm oil and add cumin seeds, mustard seeds and tumeric. After mustard seeds starts splattering, add chillies and finely cut onions and cook until golden brown. Add cut potatoes, salt, and 2 Tablespoons of water and simmer. Mix separately flour in 1/4 cup water (blend) and add to the above mixture and boil on low flame. Serve hot.

Jam also will hold its shape, but it is less firm than jelly. Jam is made from crushed or chopped fruits and sugar. Jams made from a mixture of fruits are usually called conserves, especially when they include citrus fruits, nuts, raisins, or coconut. Preserves are made of small, whole fruits or uniform-size pieces of fruits in a clear, thick, slightly jellied syrup. Marmalades are soft fruit jellies with small pieces of fruit or citrus peel evenly suspended in a transparent jelly. Fruit butters are made from fruit pulp cooked with sugar until thickened to a spreadable consistency. To learn how to preserve fruits by canning, read the free instruction booklets provided by makers of canning jars and supplies.

Drying Food

Preserving food by drying is the oldest method of food preservation. Sun drying of fruits and vegetables was practiced before biblical times by Chinese, Hindus, Persians, Greeks and Egyptians. Dried foods have the advantages of taking up very little space, not requiring refrigeration and providing variety to the diet. They are good for backpacking, lunches, camping, and snacks in general.

Drying is a comparatively simple process, requiring little outlay of equipment, time and money. Even though drying is not difficult, it does take time, constant attention, skill, and understanding of the principles of food drying methods.

Preserving food requires the control of enzymes and microorganisms. Microorganisms which grow rapidly on raw or fresh food products can be controlled by drying because the lack of water limits the growth of microorganisms; however, drying does not kill the microorganisms. Inactivation of enzymes in the fruit or vegetable is usually controlled by a pretreatment. Enzymes can catalyze undesirable flavor and color changes.

Nutritional Value of Dried Fruits and Vegetables

Calories: No change. The calorie content of the dried food, however, will be higher per unit of weight because nutrients become more concentrated as water is removed.

Fiber: No change

Minerals: Some may be lost in soaking, but no data are available. None is lost in the drying process.

Vitamins: Those most often found in fruit and vegetables are A, C and the B vitamins. If vegetables are blanched, vitamin A activity is maintained to a high degree. Losses of vitamin C vary widely depending on treatment. Speed in drying and absence of sunlight are advantages in maintaining ascorbic acid as is decreasing the air temperatures as complete dryness is approached. Only moderate losses of B vitamins occur during drying.

Yields

Because drying removes moisture, the food shrinks and decreases in size and weight, thus requiring less space for storage. When water is added to the dried product, it returns to its original size. Yields of dried products are directly related to how much water is in the original product. Twenty-five pounds of apples will yield about 4 pounds of dried apples. Twenty-five pounds of onions will yield about 3 pounds of dried onions.

Fruits and vegetables selected for drying should be sound, fresh, and in the "peak" of condition; ripe, but still firm and at the right state of maturity. Wilted or inferior material will not make a satisfactory product. Immature fruits will be weak in color and flavor. Over-mature vegetables are usually tough and woody. Over-mature or bruised fruits are likely to spoil before the drying process can be accomplished. Fruit and vegetables that are inferior before drying will be inferior after drying.

Heat is supplied by the sun or electrical heat. If the drying temperature is too low, the product will sour. Drying should be done as quickly as possible, at a temperature that does not seriously affect the texture, color, and flavor of the fruit or vegetable. If the temperature is too high or the humidity too low, there is a danger of moisture being removed too fast. This can cause a hardening of the outer cells of the product (case hardening) which prevents water vapor from diffusing from the inner cells. Drying is best accomplished when the process is continuous. When heat is applied intermittently, temperatures conducive to bacterial growth can develop.

Each piece of food should have good exposure to air. Food should be only one layer deep with space around it. This space does not need to be large since the product will shrink during the drying process. A good flow of air is necessary. The air will absorb all the moisture it can hold; therefore, fresh air should be forced to circulate to remove water vapor and carry moisture away from the food being dried. The force of the circulating air should not be so strong that it can blow the dried food off the rack.

Methods of Drying

There are three methods commonly used for home drying: sun drying, oven drying, and cabinet-type dryers with controlled heat and air circulation (referred to herein as dehydrators). Whatever the method used, the prepared food should be placed carefully on trays so that air can circulate around the product and between the trays.

Sun Drying

Sun drying is the evaporation of water from products by sun or solar heat, assisted by movement of surrounding air. To be successful, it demands a rainless season of bright sunshine and temperatures above 98°F coinciding with the period of product maturity. Sun drying requires considerable care. Products must be protected from insects and must be sheltered during the night. This method is relatively slow, because the sun does not cause rapid evaporation of moisture. Reduced drying times may be achieved by using a solar dryer.

To Sun Dry Fruit

After fruit has been treated, place on trays one layer deep. Air circulation below as well as above fruit will speed up drying time.

Solar Dryer

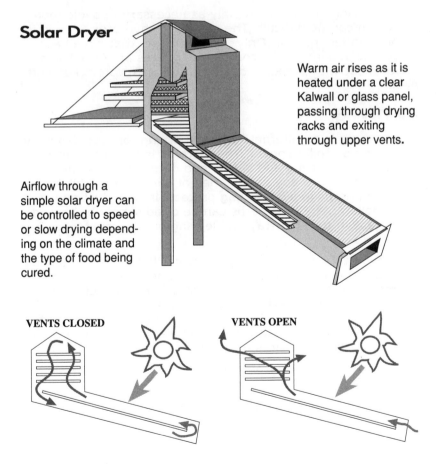

Warm air rises as it is heated under a clear Kalwall or glass panel, passing through drying racks and exiting through upper vents.

Airflow through a simple solar dryer can be controlled to speed or slow drying depending on the climate and the type of food being cured.

VENTS CLOSED

VENTS OPEN

Place in direct sun, turn occasionally. A light covering of cheesecloth or screen suspended above the food will keep it from insects. Place table legs in cans of water to prevent insects from crawling up into the food.

Several days in direct sun are sufficient to make fruit about two-thirds dry. At this stage, stack the trays in the shade where there is good air circulation and continue drying until leathery.

To Sun Dry Vegetables

Spread in thin layer on trays. Place in the direct sun, turn occasionally. Too much direct sun on vegetables can cause sunburn or scorching. Drying can be completed in the shade.

Beans and peas that are allowed to dry on the vine need to undergo a pasteurization process for insect control. Freeze 48 hours, or spread the dried product one layer thick and heat in a 150°F oven for 30 minutes.

Sun drying of meat as rapidly as necessary to avoid food poisoning can be difficult. The use of a dehydrator or oven is recommended instead. Only sun dry meats that have been treated with curing salts containing nitrates and/or nitrites. Cover meat with suspended cheesecloth or mesh to keep off flies.

Air Drying

Air drying is an alternative to sun drying for such products as herbs and chili peppers. The material is tied into bunches or strung on a string and suspended out of the sun until dry. This can be in a shady porch, shed or corner of the kitchen. Enclosing herbs in a paper bag protects it from dust and other pollutants. Some herbs can be dried simply by spreading on a dish towel or tray and leaving on the counter for 2 or 3 days.

Dehydrators with thermostatic controlled heat and forced air circulation are available from a number of commercial sources. They can also be constructed from a variety of materials available to the home carpenter. Dehydrators require: 1) an enclosed cabinet, 2) a controlled source of heat, and 3) forced air to carry away the moisture. Venting to allow intake and exhaust of air is necessary.

Place a thermometer on one of the shelves inside your working dehydrator. Desirable dryer temperatures are 140 to 160°F. Controls to adjust temperature should be accurate. Uniformity of temperature inside the dehydrator is important if you wish to avoid having to rotate shelves during the drying procedure. Temperature uniformity can be measured by checking the temperature front and back, top and bottom.

The air flow through the dehydrator is also important. Designs of dehydrators vary but all will have an air intake and exhaust. The intake for air is frequently on the bottom or back and the exhaust on the top or front of the dehydrator. With the dehydrator turned on, light a match or a candle and holding it in the outflow of air slowly move it toward the dehydrator. The air flow should blow it out at 2-4 feet from the exit port.

Oven Drying

Oven drying is harder to control than drying with a dehydrator; however some products can be quite successfully dried in the oven. It typically takes two to three times longer to dry food in an oven. Thus, the oven is not as efficient and uses more energy.

Set the oven at the lowest setting, preferably around 150°F, and leave the door open 2 to 3 inches (block open if necessary). A small fan positioned to the side of the oven door blowing inward will help remove moist air.

CAUTION: This can be hazardous in a home with small children. Convection ovens already have a built-in fan system.

Crazing

Some fruits (such as prunes, plums, cranberries, blueberries, and grapes) have a natural protective wax coating. If they are to be dried whole, it is best if these fruits are pretreated by dipping them in boiling water for 15-60 seconds according to the size and toughness of the skin, and then immediately dipping them in cold water. This process crazes the wax coating on the skin and allows the moisture to escape, thus speeding the drying time of the fruit. Unlike blanching, it is not desirable to have the heat penetrate to the center of the product.

Ascorbic Acid

Pure crystalline ascorbic acid is a good antioxidant, but sometimes difficult to find. It is available through drugstores or chemical companies. For apples, dissolve 2 1/2 teaspoons of crystalline ascorbic acid in each cup of cold water. For peaches, apricots, and pears, dissolve 1 teaspoon of ascorbic acid in each cup of cold water. One cup of solution will treat about 5 quarts of cut fruit. As the fruit is prepared (peeled, diced, sliced, etc.), place it in a large (1 gal.) plastic bag. Add the ascorbic acid solution. Shake thoroughly so that all

Boston Beans

4 to 6 servings

2 cans pinto beans or 4 cups cooked beans
1/4 cup molasses
1/4 cup brown sugar
1/4 cup ketchup
2 Tablespoons prepared mustard
1 teaspoon onion powder
1/2 teaspoon garlic powder
Combine all ingredients and cook until bubbling hot.

Bean Burgers

makes 8 patties

15 oz. can kidney beans, drained
2 cups cooked rice
1/4 cup finely chopped onion
2 Tablespoons ketchup
1 teaspoon dried oregano
1 teaspoon poultry seasoning
1/2 teaspoon salt, dash pepper
Mash the beans, mash in the rice, onion, ketchup and season-ings. Wet hands and shape into 8 patties, about 1/2 inch thick. Heat a skillet and brown patties in a little oil.

Bean Burritos

4 servings

4 ten-inch tortillas
2 cups Refried Beans
Cook tortillas about 1 minute on each side. Heat beans, divide into the middle of the tortillas, fold envelope-style around the beans. Serve with salsa.

Refried Beans (Frijoles)

1 medium onion, chopped
1 Tablespoon canola oil
1 Tablespoon chili powder
2 teaspoons cumin powder
1 15-oz. can pintos, red kidney or black beans, drained
Heat a pan and fry the onion in oil until soft. Stir in chili and cumin. Add the beans and mash with a potato masher until smooth. Add a little crushed red pepper flakes, if desired.

Pinto Beans with Chutney

2 cans pinto beans, drained
1/2 cup onion, finely chopped
1 1/2 teaspoon dry mustard
1/4 cup honey
1/4 cup chutney, chopped
Combine all ingredients and
simmer until heated through.

parts of the fruit are coated with the ascorbic acid solution. Drain well.

Ascorbic acid powders contain ascorbic acid and are found in grocery stores for use on "fresh fruit." They do not work as effectively as pure ascorbic acid. Follow the directions on the package.

Fruit juice dips

Soaking the fruits in a fruit juice naturally containing ascorbic acid will help keep the natural color and prevent further darkening. These will also add their flavor to the product. Soak the fruit pieces 3-5 minutes, remove and drain well. Only use the juice twice before replacing. (The juice can be consumed.) Possible juices include orange, grapefruit, lemon, lime, or pineapple juice.

Vitamin C tablets

Crush to a powder and mix 1 teaspoon of 500 mg vitamin C tablets with 1 quart of water. Vitamin C tablets contain carriers which do not dissolve as well as pure crystalline ascorbic acid and may result in harmless white particles floating on the solution. Soak the fruit in the solution for 3-5 minutes.

Other Treatments

Saline
Soak sliced fresh produce in salt water solution (4–6 Tbsp. salt to 1 gal. water) for 10 min.
Honey dip
Dissolve 1/2 cup sugar in 1 1/2 cups boiling water. Add 1/2 cup honey. Makes 2 cups. Dip fruit in small batches. Allow fruit to soak 3 to 5 minutes. Remove with slotted spoon and drain.
Honey lemon dip
Slightly heat and dissolve 1/2 cup of honey with the juice of one lemon in 1/2 cup of water. Dip the fruit, then spread on drying trays.
Hot syrup
Combine one cup each of corn syrup, sugar and water. Bring to boil. Add fruit. Simmer 10-15 minutes. Drain well. Place on trays sprayed with oil to avoid sticking of fruit. Lift fruit gently from pan to tray. Syrup dip will increase the drying time. The final product is like a candied fruit.

Drying Vegetables

Only fresh vegetables in prime condition can produce a good quality dried product. Wilted ones should not be used— deterioration has already begun. One moldy bean may give a bad flavor to an entire lot. If possible, gather the vegetables early in the morning, and start the drying process as soon as possible.

General procedure

SORT - Carefully discard any bruised or undesirable product
WASH - Carefully and thoroughly
PEEL - Slice according to recipe
TREAT - All vegetables, with the exception of onions, garlic, horseradish and herbs, by blanching
BLANCH - Drop pieces of vegetables into boiling, salted water and boil for 1 to 2 minutes, drain and put in cold water to stop the cooking process. Blanching preserves flavor and color
DRY - Spread one layer thick on racks and dry

For adjustable dehydrators, set temperature at 140°F. Sun drying requires temperatures of 98°F or above.

Fruit Leathers

Fruit leathers provide nourishing snacks and are easy to prepare. This product can be made by pureeing fruit, either fresh or a drained, canned product.

To make leathers:

1. Wash fresh fruit and peel if desired. Remove pits and seeds. Slice or cube if the fruit is large.

2. Make a puree from the desired fruit. A blender or food processor can be used on fresh or precooked fruit. If a blender is to be used for fresh fruit, puree the fruit first and then bring the puree to a boil while stirring continuously. If a food mill or potato masher is to be used, it is best to cook fresh fruit with a small amount of water in a covered pan until tender first, then puree the fruit. The heat process will inactivate enzymes that can cause the leather to discolor. Canned fruit should be well drained. It is not necessary to heat canned fruit. The pureed product can be lightly sweetened if desired. Heavily sweetened fruits will remain sticky and will not dry well.

3. Spread the puree in a thin layer on a plastic film. The plastic film can be on a cookie sheet, a pizza pan, an oven-safe dinner plate or on some dehydrator racks. Make sure that the plastic sheet edges do not fold over and cover any of the puree. The puree should be about 1/4 inch deep.

4. Dry the leather in a dehydrator or oven. The leather is adequately dried when you can peel it from the plastic. The dried product should have a bright translucent appearance, chewy texture, and a good fruit flavor.

5. Leathers can be stored by rolling them up while they are still on the film and placed in a glass jar with a tight lid or in a plastic bag. They retain their color and flavor for several months at room temperature, but storage life can be extended by refrigeration or freezing.

Drying of Herbs/Seasonings

Mint, oregano, basil, parsley, tarragon, sage, thyme, marjoram, rosemary: gather when plant begins to flower, but the leaves are still green and tender. The young leaves at the tip of the plant are the most flavorful. They are least bitter if gathered in early morning. Remove blemished or dirty leaves, tie together in 4-5 inch bunches and hang upside down inside a paper bag in a warm, dry place where they will not be in direct sunlight, or spread on a dish towel or screen rack. After drying, remove leaves from stems and store in airtight container. Drying will take a few days in open air, or 2 weeks in the paper bag. They should flake to the touch when dried.

Chives: Chop into the size pieces desired. Spread on a plate or cookie sheet and set out of the way in a warm room.

Dill seeds and other seeds: Spread on plate or screens and dry indoors.

Horseradish: Remove small rootlets, stubs. Peel or scrape roots. Grate then spread thin on trays and dry in dehydrator.

Garlic: Peel cloves. Slice or chop. Dry in a dehydrator, or if finely chopped, spread on plate or screen and dry at room temperature.

Citrus peel: Wash thoroughly. Remove outer 1/16 to 1/8 inch of peel and dry this portion. Avoid white bitter pith. Outer portion can be grated or sliced from fruit. Spread on plate.

How to Vacuum Pack Dried Produce

Fill canning jars with dried fruit. With lid lightly screwed down, place jars in oven at 325°F for 15 minutes. Tighten lid when removed from oven. Test the lids on the dried fruit after it has cooled to see that you do have a vacuum seal. Never vacuum pack your dried vegetable unless you know they are truly dry, either by drying to a brittle stage or by calculation. For vegetables, dry to 90% solids level.

Conditioning or Curing of Dried Foods

Pieces of food taken from the drying trays are not always uniformly dry. To condition, place cooled dried fruit loosely in large plastic or glass containers, about two-thirds full. Cover with a cloth and store in a warm, dry well-ventilated place. Stir and feel the food every day for a week. If there is evidence of moisture, return the food to the dryer. The food can be left in this way for one to two weeks. This assures an even distribution of moisture and reduces the chance of spoilage in the product. If you dried the produce to a calculated final solids content, you can package without the conditioning step. Variations in moisture content will equalize between the pieces in the package.

Foods exposed to insects before or during the drying process should be pasteurized to destroy insect eggs. Preheat oven to 175°F. Spread the food loosely, not more than 1 inch deep, on trays. Do not put more than two trays in the oven at once. Heat brittle, dried vegetables for 10 minutes; heat fruits 15 minutes. Oven pasteurizing results in additional loss of vitamins, and may scorch food.

Freezer method: Seal dried food in heavy freezer containers (bags or boxes). Freeze for 48 hours to kill insects and insect eggs. Remove and let reach room temperature before packaging for permanent storage.

> Bay leaves will also deter insects. Buy an ounce of dried bay leaves at a health food store and as soon as you open a package of flour or grain, place one or two bay leaves in the package. Scatter extra leaves on pantry shelves. Freshen leaves monthly.

Shelf Life

Dried products will keep for a year or more if sealed in moistureproof containers and stored in a cool, dark, dry place. Heat and light have an adverse effect on the quality of dried foods. Dried foods must be protected from moisture absorption and from insect infestation. Glass jars, tin cans with tight-fitting lids and plastic containers are all satisfactory containers storing dried foods. Containers should be filled as full as possible without crushing.

Remember: first in, first out (FIFO). Even if a product is not at the end of its shelf life, use it when the need arises and then replace it with a fresher one.

Beans

Canned beans need only be heated, or taken right from the can for salads. Dried beans need to be sorted, with shrivelled and spotted beans removed, then washed and soaked. They can be slow cooked in a Dutch oven over a fireplace or woodstove or in a pressure cooker.

Pressure Cooker

A pressure cooker will save time and energy in cooking beans. Never fill the cooker more than about one-third of capacity to allow for expansion and foaming. The foaming can be minimized by adding 1 tablespoon of oil. Approximate cooking time at 10 pounds of pressure is 20 minutes, at 15 pounds of pressure, 10 minutes. Never pressure cook split peas or lentils.

Red Beans and Rice

4 to 6 servings

Cook 1 cup rice.
1 large onion, chopped
1 Tablespoon oil
1/2 teaspoon salt
2 teaspoons chili powder
15 oz. can red kidney beans, drained
1 cup salsa or picante sauce
Fry the onion in the oil, add salt and chili powder. Add beans and salsa to onions, sir in the rice, heat through.

Black Bean Stew

4 servings

1 cup chopped onion
1 Tablespoon oil
3 cloves garlic
1 teaspoon salt
2 potatoes, cut up
2 carrots, sliced
3 cups vegetable broth
1 15 oz. can black beans
1 Tablespoons dried parsley
Fry the onion in oil, add garlic and salt. Add potatoes, carrots and broth. Simmer until vegetables are tender. Stir in beans and parsley, bring to a boil, serve hot. Use fresh parsley or coriander if you have it in your garden or windowbox.

Bean Preparation Timetable

	Soaked, open-kettle	No soak and pressure cook	Soak and pressure cook	Yields per 2 cups dry
adzuki	30 min	15 min	5-10 min	6 2/3
anasazi	60 min	25 min	15 min	5
black	90 min	30-35 min	20 min	5
black-eyed peas	25 min	10 min	5-8 min	4 3/4
garbanzo	4 hr 25 min	35 min	25 min	5
Great Northern	90 min	25 min	20 min	5
kidney	35-40 min	30 min	15-20 min	4 1/2
lentil, brown*	20-25 min	**	**	5
lentil, orange*	15-20 min	**	**	3 1/3
lima, baby	30 min	10-15 min	8 min	4
navy	35-40 min	22 min	15 min	5
pinto	90 min	35-40 min	20-25 min	5
soybeans	**	60 min	45 min	4
split peas*	75-90 min	7 min	**	4

* It is not necessary to presoak lentils and split peas.
** Do not use this method for this variety of beans.

This table courtesy of Barb Bloomfield, author of *Fabulous Beans* (Summertown, Tenn.: Book Publishing Company, 1994).

Textured Vegetable Protein (TVP)

Textured vegetable protein or TVP is made from soybeans after the oil is extracted. You may know this nutritious product as seasoned "bacon bits" or "hamburger helper." It's available in granules or chunks in many different flavors from the Mail Order Catalog (1-800-695-2241). Pour 7/8 cup of hot water over 1 cup granules to reconstitute, then use in recipes as you'd use ground meat. It has a long shelf life.

"Sausage" TVP
6 servings

1 cup TVP
7/8 cup hot water
1 teaspoon each sage and thyme
1 teaspoon onion powder
1 teaspoon salt
1/4 teaspoon black pepper
2 Tablespoons canola oil

Pour hot water over TVP and let stand 10 minutes. Stir in seasonings. Heat a pan, add oil, fry TVP until lightly browned. Add to Country Gravy.

Country Sausage Gravy
6 servings

3 Tablespoons canola oil
1/4 cup unbleached flour
2 cups reconstituted dried milk
1 teaspoon salt
1/4 teaspoon black pepper
1 teaspoon sage
1 teaspoon thyme
1 teaspoon onion powder
Browned TVP sausage

Stir oil and flour together in a 2-quart pan. Stir in milk, salt and pepper. Whisk until bubbly. Whisk in seasonings. Add browned sausage last. Serve with biscuits or potatoes.

Potato Hash with TVP
6 servings

1/2 cup TVP granules
1/3 cup hot water
1 Tablespoon soy sauce
3 large potatoes, grated
1 small onion, chopped
1 teaspoon salt
2 Tablespoons canola oil

Mix hot water, soy sauce and TVP let stand 10 minutes. Mix with potatoes, onions and salt. Heat skillet, add oil and fry hash until lightly browned and potatoes are tender, turning as it browns.

Rice

Rice is a versatile, economical food for family meals. It is a good source of energy, and can supply vitamins and minerals to the diet. Even though there are 7,000 varieties of rice produced in the world, the consumer needs to be aware that generally there are only three different lengths of rice grain and five different kinds.

Long grain rice is distinguished because its length is four to five times its width. The grains are clear and translucent. The grains remain distinct and separate after cooking. Medium grain rice is about three times as long as its width. This type is less expensive than long grain rice. This is due to the fact that it requires a shorter growing season and produces a higher yield per acre. It is also easier to mill than the long grained variety. Short grain rice is only one and a half to two times as long as it is wide. It is generally the least expensive of the three lengths.

With many different kinds of rice to select from, it is important to be able to distinguish between the different varieties available.

Rice Preparation Timetable

Rice Variety	Water	Salt	Cooking Time	Yield
1 cup brown	2 1/2 cups	1 tsp.	45 min.	4 cups
1 cup white	2 cups	1 tsp.	14 min.	3 cups
1 cup parboiled (converted)	2 1/4 cups	1 tsp.	20 min.	3 1/4 cups
1 cup instant	1 cup	1/2 tsp.	Do not boil. 5 min. in hot water	2 cups

Time may need to be lengthened due to altitude.

Brown rice is the whole, unpolished grain of rice with the outer fibrous, inedible hull removed. Brown rice requires more water and longer cooking time than white rice. It has a delightful, chewy texture, with a distinctive nut-like flavor.

Regular milled white rice is rice from which hulls, germ, outer bran layers and most of the inner bran are removed in the milling process. The grains are bland in flavor and are fluffy and distinct when cooking directions are followed.

Parboiled rice—sometimes called processed or converted rice—has been treated to keep some of the natural vitamins and minerals the whole grain contains. It has been cooked

Conserving Water

Have on hand some Boil-in-a-Bag rice. Measure a quart of water into a coffee pot or chafing dish. When it is boiling, drop in the package of rice and cook for the prescribed minutes. Remove the rice and you will have about 2 1/2 cups of hot water left that you can use to make instant coffee or hot tea.

NoCook Peanut Sauce for Rice   **4 servings**

4 Tablespoons peanut butter
3 Tablespoons soy sauce
3 Tablespoons balsamic vinegar
3 cloves garlic, chopped
1/2 to 1 teaspoon cayenne pepper
1/2 cup boiling water
Mix peanut butter, soy sauce, vinegar, garlic, pepper in a bowl. Pour hot water over to thin down and let stand 1 minute.

Fried Rice   **6 servings**

1 onion, chopped
2 Tablespoons canola oil
2 cups cabbage, shredded
1 carrot, grated
1 teaspoon salt
3 to 4 cups cooked rice
2 Tablespoons soy sauce
1 7 oz can water chestnuts, sliced (optional)
Fry the onion in the oil about 5 minutes, add cabbage, carrot and salt. Cook 5 to 10 minutes, stir in rice and soy sauce.

Spanish Rice   **4 servings**

1 onion, chopped
1 Tablespoon canola oil
1 7 oz. can green chilies
1 15 oz. can tomatoes, chopped
3 cups cooked rice, cooled
Hot sauce to taste
Fry the onions in the oil, add chopped chilies and tomatoes. Stir in the cooked rice. Add hot sauce to taste.

---

before packaging by a special steam pressure process. It requires longer cooking time than regular milled white rice, but after cooking the grains are fluffy, separate and plump.

Precooked rice—quick type—is completely cooked. It needs only to stand in boiling water to be ready for serving. Cooking this product will result in a gummy, indistinguishable mass.

Fortified or Enriched rice: This product is a combination of highly fortified rice with ordinary milled rice. A coating of vitamins and minerals—thiamine, niacin, iron, and sometimes riboflavin—is used to fortify rice. This coating adheres to the rice and does not dissolve with ordinary washing or cooking.

Wild rice is not rice at all, but the seed of a wild water grass found around the Great Lakes region. It is much more expensive than the types of rice described above. Many Americans have discovered this rice and developed a taste for it. The demand for it is almost greater than the supply.

Some rules are a MUST in preparing rice. Due to the fact that the B vitamins are added to rice in the form of powder, much of the valuable nutrients are lost if the product is not handled properly.

- Except where a recipe calls for it, do not wash rice before cooking, or rinse it after cooking. Rice is one of the most sanitary foods. Rice grown and milled in the U.S. is clean. Nutrients on the surface of the rice are washed away if it is washed or rinsed before cooking.
- Do not use too much water when cooking rice. Any water drained off means wasted food value. Too much water makes soggy rice. Too little water results in a dry product.
- Do not peek when cooking rice. Lifting the lid lets out steam and lowers the temperature.
- Do not stir rice after it comes to a boil. This breaks up the grains; makes rice gummy.
- Do not leave rice in a pan in which it is cooked for more than 5 to 10 minutes or the cooked rice will pack.

Easy Rice Pudding
6 servings

1/4 teaspoon salt
2 cups water
1/2 cup uncooked white rice
1/2 cup raisins
1/4 cup nonfat dry milk
1/2 cup sugar
1 cup water
1 1/4 teaspoon vanilla
Cinnamon or nutmeg, if desired

Rinse rice. Add salt to water, bring to a boil, and stir rice into boiling water. Bring back to boiling point and lower heat until the water is just bubbling. Add raisins, cover tightly and cook slowly for 20 minutes. Combine dry milk and sugar, stir into water until mixed. Stir into rice, add vanilla. Simmer 10 minutes or until flavors are blended. Chill. Serve sprinkled lightly with cinnamon or nutmeg, if desired.

"If life is a process of discovering who we are, Y2K is when we find out."
—Tom Atlee, Co-Intelligence Institute

*"The public faces a high risk that critical services provided by
the government and the private sector could be severely
disrupted by the year 2000 computing crisis. Financial
transactions could be delayed, flights grounded, power lost,
and national defense affected."*
General Accounting Office, U.S. Congress

Step 7. Enjoy Yourself

I f you find yourself cut off from telephones, electricity,
rapid transit, or other comforts and conveniences which
we had come to expect in the late 20th Century, it is still
possible to enjoy yourself.

Bring along some books or games to wherever you are
sheltered. If you find yourself out of work for days or weeks,
recognize it as the blessing that it is. This might be that time
you have been waiting for to write a great novel, catch up on
your pleasure reading, or do some outdoor walking.

During any sort of an emergency, information becomes
extremely important. Make sure you have a portable battery-operated AM/FM radio with good reception, and enough
battery power to last at least a week of continuous play. You
can time how long the radio will operate and buy batteries
accordingly.

The BayGen radio ($99.95 from Radioland) needs no
batteries and gives 30 minutes of sound on 30 seconds of
cranking. Useful accessories include an LED light, solar
battery charger, and shortwave antenna.

If a family member will be away for more than a couple of
hours, they should have a means to communicate with you
(i.e., walkie-talkie, CB).

Entertainment systems, walkmans, VCR's, etc., may or
may not be affected directly by Y2K problems, but make
sure they can run on batteries. Also make sure you have a
few simple (nonelectronic) instruments—like guitars, flutes
and drums—around for fun.

Children

Well before disaster strikes, consider how your children might react to sudden change in their environment, not to mention what your own reactions might be. How might a crisis affect each person's emotional and physical well being?

The best way to build confidence is to make a plan. Discuss the plan with your family members. You can treat emergency situations as an unplanned camp out, but tell children simply and matter-of-factly about the problem and how it is to be handled.

Coping With Emotions

Remember that children mirror their parents anxieties. To reduce your childrens' fears, be calm yourself. In a bad situation a child may exhibit unusually childish behavior. Most children are not capable of understanding the magnitude and severity of a crisis. Be understanding and patient. Use a familiar toy or book to provide comfort.

If your child's behavior appears unusual, he or she may have lost something. Maybe a pet or favorite toy. Ask the child regardless of age what he or she misses and try to replace the lost belonging.

Older Adults

If you have older or disabled relatives living at home, review emergency procedures with them. If you need special transportation or assistance, try to arrange these in advance. If a relative lives in an nursing home, discuss emergency preparedness with the staff and plan accordingly.

Providing Support

People who experience a serious loss, such as a death or major injury go through a grieving process. It is important to be available during this period, and also to provide support after the crisis is over. At these times, when the crisis has passed and other people have returned to their routines, feelings of sadness and aloneness are often greatest.

One of the most effective ways of helping is to look positively at even the most difficult situations. Childre and Cryer suggest that in a crisis situation, stop, look and listen to whatever internal program you are experiencing so that you can evaluate your situation with more clarity. You know what your TV looks like when you press the pause button on the VCR. To pause your present reality, become still inside and frame the moment. Then look to your heart to gain the objectivity and clarity you need.

Even without the strain of Y2K, many people are already feeling overstressed and on the edge of personal chaos. Achieving coherent communication in an increasingly noisy world is important.

Y2K challenges our society to become even more adaptable and resilient at a time when a "bunker mentality" could seem quite reasonable. We must be aware there will be life after Y2K. We can grow in experience and friendships through this crisis.

In any planning sessions surrounding your personal or organizational response to Y2K, keep the emotional volume to a minimum. This principle is particularly essential in the area of communication. As the typical media frenzy to uncover the next stimulating story really catches on to Y2K, we could be in for a wild ride. Here are some essential points to reflect on:

- Reduce emotionalism in all Y2K-related communication.
- Avoid feeding paranoia, fear and anxiety while keeping realistic, balanced perspectives.
- Be authentic in telling the story, as best you know it.

Certain key elements can keep attitudes and energy high. The lack of these prepare the environment for an outbreak of what has been called the emotional virus. Many researchers have looked at what makes social climates strong and resilient. Invariably the common factors involve the following:

- Contribution—the sense that the contribution one makes is worthwhile
- Recognition—the feeling that one's contribution is recognized and appreciated
- Clarity—the degree of clarity about what is expected of an individual
- Self-expression—feeling free to question the way things are done
- Challenge—feeling that one's work is challenging
- Supportive management—the extent to which people feel supported by their immediate manager

In many catastrophes, a quiet emotional virus starts to take hold, feeding off the fear and strain of the individuals struggling to make headway and stay balanced. Emotional viruses are created by individual immaturity and group stress. As with other viruses, an emotional virus can be highly infectious. But there are ways to resist.

Teams of people who function at high levels of creativity and collaboration are entrained. Entrainment is a term used in physics to describe the tendency of systems to synchronize to allow maximum efficiency. When a team is entrained, much more energy and innovation is unleashed than when a team is incoherent, its goals and values fuzzy, and its communication frustrated or mired in bickering. Entrained teams result when the individual members have a high degree of internal self-management and when communication is coherent and sincere.

Let's look at some activities which can build both individual and group spirit:

One of the greatest pleasures in an era before internal combustion engines and electric lights was the home garden. Providing food for your family and friends can also provide a satisfying way to spend your time.

The Home Garden

The man who seeks a comfortable living will do better to rent on long lease or buy a few acres convenient to trolley or railroad communication with a city; besides the returns which will come to the farmer from the use of a few acres, if he is the owner he will get a constant increase in the value of the land, due to the growth of the city. If the city grows out so that the land becomes too valuable to farm, he will be well paid for leaving.
  - Bolton Hall, *Three Acres and Liberty* (1907)

The things to be considered in the home garden are: (1) a sufficient product to supply the family; (2) continuous succession of crops; (3) ease and cheapness of cultivation; (4) maintenance of the productivity of the land year after year.

Where the land is favorably situated a fortune may be made in cultivation of a few acres, but if your idea of farming is to bury "some seeds" in untilled ground and wait until they come up, you will wait in vain for a decent crop.

You must cultivate with brains. The Germans say, "What your head won't do, your legs have to."

We must not put all our time into one crop because unfavorable conditions may make failures of one or more crops. In variety and succession is safety and profit. In the North, seeds of many kinds should be sown from the first of March to the first of August; in the South they should be sown every month.

By following the simple timetables for planting you will find crops maturing every month in the year. As far north as Canada you can produce cauliflower and brussels sprouts in January; kale and kohlrabi in February, lettuce and broccoli in March; spinach, endive, and radishes in April; peas, onions, and lettuce in May; asparagus and strawberries in June; beets, corn, tomatoes, cucumbers, pole and wax beans, and cabbages in July; turnips, rutabagas, escarole, chives, shallot, parsley, potatoes, peaches, and beans in August; carrots, eggplant, peppers, squash, onions and sweet potatoes in September; celery in October; cauliflower in November; and kale, kohlrabi and brussels sprouts in December.

Food for a single family can be grown in beds of any shape or size. Food for commerce or many families is best grown in rows. Even if the available area is only twenty feet wide, the rows should run lengthwise and be far enough apart (30 inches) to allow for the use of hand wheelhoes or even horse cultivators. If the rows are long, it may be necessary to grow two or three kinds of vegetables in the same row; in this case it is important that vegetables requiring the same general treatment and similar length of season be grown together. For example, a row containing parsnips and salsify, or parsnips, salsify, and late carrots would afford an ideal combination; but a row containing parsnips, cabbages, and lettuce would be problematic. All root crops might be grown on one side of the plot, all cabbage crops in the adjoining space, all tomato and eggplant crops in the center, all corn and tall things on the opposite side. Perennial crops, as asparagus and rhubarb, and gardening structures, as hotbeds and frames, should be on the border, where they will not interfere with the plowing and tilling.

Companion Crops

To get the greatest production from the soil two or more crops can be grown in the same soil at the same time—one of which will mature much earlier than the others, thereby giving its place up just about the period of growth when the second crop would need more room. This is known as companion cropping. Here are examples:

- Radishes with beets or carrots. The radishes can be harvested before the beets need the room.
- Corn with squash or pumpkin, and climbing beans in hills. These are the "three sisters" which native Americans planted.
- Early onions and cauliflower or cabbage.
- Horseradish and early cabbage.
- Lettuce with early cabbage.
- Early potatoes and early cauliflower are followed by Brussels sprouts and celery, two crops being as easily grown as one by intelligent handling.
- The best beans are grown among fruit trees.

Onion sets may be planted early in the season and onion seeds then sown. Between onion rows plant cauliflower. Later between the cauliflower, two or three cucumber seeds may be dropped. The onion sets up around the cauliflower may be taken out first, and the cauliflowers come out in time to let the cucumbers develop.

Basic Herb Dressing

Shake up in a small jar:
5 Tablespoons olive oil
2 Tablespoons red wine vinegar
1/4 teaspoon salt
1/2 teaspoon dried basil or oregano, or both
For variation add a little balsamic vinegar or a pinch of garlic powder.

Green Bean Salad   6 servings

15 ounce can French cut green beans
15 ounce can red kidney beans
15 ounce can yellow wax beans, cut
1/2 cup onion, chopped small
1/2 cup olive oil
1/4 cup red wine vinegar
2 Tablespoons sugar
Salt and pepper to taste
Drain the beans (liquids can be added to soup pot) and combine with onion in a large bowl. Whisk together the oil, vinegar and sugar, pour over beans and let stand several hours. Stir occasionally. Add salt and pepper to taste.

Black Bean Salad   4 to 5 servings

1 14-oz. can black beans, drained
2 tablespoons onion, minced
1 carrot, grated
1 Tablespoon olive oil
2 teaspoons cider vinegar
1/2 teaspoon salt
1/2 teaspoon dried basil
1/8 teaspoon black pepper
Mix oil, vinegar and spices. Stir in beans, onions, carrots.

Midway between the rows of onions grown from seeds, we can plant radishes, lettuce, herbs, spinach, or other early salad greens, which will have ample time to grow and be harvested before shading the onions. When the onions are well grown, turnips can be sown midway between their rows.

Weeds won't have much chance in a garden of this type.

In truth, what an acre may produce depends on time, place, and circumstances. Good land cultivated with good management for a term of years can provide a very comfortable living. While less favored acres could be made to produce as much, the distance to market, or market variations, might still make farming unprofitable.

For the beginner who wants to get fresh vegetables and fruits from May until midwinter, a space 100 X 200 feet is enough to feed a family.

1. Plant or cover all bare ground to avoid weeds.

2. Plant vegetables that mature at the same time near one another to make harvesting easier.

3. Plant vegetables of the same height near together—tall ones to the back.

4. Run the rows the short way, for convenience in cultivation and because one hundred feet of anything is enough.

5. Put the permanent vegetables (asparagus, rhubarb, sweet herbs) at one side, so that the rest will be easy to plow.

6. Practice rotation. Do not put vines where they were last. Put corn in a different place. The other important groups for rotation are root crops (including potatoes and

---

Chick Peas with Roasted Peppers   4 servings

16 ounce can garbanzo beans or chick peas, drained
10 or 12 ounce jar roasted red peppers, with liquid
2 Tablespoons minced onion
1 Tablespoon extra-virgin olive oil
2 teaspoons lemon juice or rice vinegar
Combine ingredients in a glass bowl, adding a little salt and pepper to taste if desired.

Pineapple-Beet Salad   4 to 6 servings

15-oz. can diced beets, drained
1 small can pineapple tidbits
Mix together for a delicious salad.

---

onions); cabbage tribe, peas and beans, tomatoes, eggplant and peppers, salad plants.

By training on trellis or wire, the smaller fruit plantings can be made much closer.

If fruits are wanted in the garden, plant a row of apple trees along the northern border, plums and pears on the western sides, cherries and peaches on the eastern side. Next to the apple trees run a grape trellis; and then in succession east and west, run blackberries, raspberries, gooseberries, and currants. These rows, with the apple trees, form a windbreak, and besides adding to variety, protect your vegetables. Next to the bush fruits, between them and at ends of the vegetable rows, put rhubarb, asparagus, and strawberries.

Insect pests must be watched for and their destructive work checked. Ashes, slaked lime, or any kind of dust or powder destroy most insects which prey on the leaves of plants. The reason for this is that the dust closes the pores through which the insects breathe. It should therefore be applied when the leaves are dry.

Chickens given access to the garden for brief times (but never when new plants are just appearing) will gather up insects and deter their reproduction. Marigolds will also deter many insects from settling in.

Special crops require special tools. In general, you should have a hand-pruner, wheelbarrow, digging spade, fork, hoe, watering can, rake, hose and sprayer. The wheel hoe is a great saver—of backache—especially to the beginner. A scythe is good to keep weeds away from fences. A sickle is handy to keep down grass and we prefer Japanese sickles for their superior design and maneuverability. A weed whip has a zigzag blade for cutting off young weeds which are just starting above ground. It is pushed backward and forward and cuts both ways. It is very good for soft ground. Extra spades, hoes, a post-hole digger, sledge hammer, and trowels will all come in handy at some point. Make a shelter for your machines and tools or they will rust through the winter. Many farmers, through neglect, have to replace their tool equipment every four or five years, but with attention and care, the original equipment still ought to be in use in twenty years.

Tractors

If you want to get mechanized, before investing in a riding tractor consider a walk-behind machine like a rototiller or Gravely Tractor. Gravely's Two-Wheel Tractors are designed for both commercial users and homeowners with serious farming in mind. Engineered with all-gear direct drive, Gravelys will perform on any terrain because of their low center of gravity. With over 20 quick-mounting, custom-engineered attachments, these tractors can handle virtually any small tractor job—mowing, excavating, tilling, snowblowing, and plowing.

If you have a short- or medium-term need for a dedicated tractor, you may want buy and then resell a used machine when you're finished with it. After several years, heavy duty tractors in good condition do not depreciate much in value. In fact, some "classic" 40-50 year old tractors, like the Ford "N" series, now sell for more than they cost when they were new! As with any used machine, make very sure it is in good condition when you buy it, take care of it while you own it (be prepared to make some repairs). How much you can resell it for depends on finding a buyer who appreciates its value.

Instead of buying, consider renting machinery or implements you need only occasionally. Many equipment dealers rent anything from single bottom plows to tractor/loader/backhoes. Rental fees are usually reasonable—especially compared to the purchase price—most places offer delivery and pickup of large equipment and, except for very large equipment, do not require an operator's license.

The skid loader, or skid steer vehicle, has replaced the tractor for many commercial, agricultural and landscaping applications. An excellent machine for everything from cleaning out barns to excavating, the skid loader can be equipped with a variety of implements, including backhoe, brush cutter, post hole digger, manure forks, tiller, trencher, hay spear and even tank-like tracks. Because of its narrow width, tight turning radius and quick agility, a skid loader is ideal for working in tight areas. But for lawn mowing and general field work (plowing, baling, raking, planting), a tractor is more useful.

If you already own or are thinking of purchasing an all-terrain vehicle (ATV) you may be surprised to learn how many attachments are available for it. Snow plows and self-powered mowers, brush cutters and tillers are all available for pushing or towing with an ATV.

Borrowing tools or equipment from friends, relatives or neighbors is still acceptable behavior in some parts of the country. You should, of course, be willing to reciprocate, should the need for one of your tools ever arise. Also, you should try to return the item in better condition than when you borrowed it. Have it repaired or replace it if it breaks while you have it (even if it wasn't your fault that it broke), return it shortly after you borrowed it and remember to say, "thank you."

Try bartering a service you can perform in exchange for someone else's service to you. Find someone with the equipment you need who is able to do the job for you and see if you can perform an equal-value service of some kind for him or her.

Permaculture (for permanent agriculture) is a design science of sustainable living. We strongly recommend finding a permaculture instructor and taking the design course. In a short amount of time you can gain food, water and financial security from very small investments of money and labor.

Soil Fertility

To get a garden fully established on new land requires two or three years. Worn-out land takes longer to build the high fertility needed for maximum production. Crops like asparagus and rhubarb take two years to establish. Bush fruits take three years. Fruit trees take even longer to get maximum results.

When land is cropped every season, the nitrogen, potash, and phosphorus removed from the soil must be replaced in some form, otherwise you have diminishing returns, while the expense for labor is the same. In farming small areas for specialties you cannot easily invoke the principle of rotation by enriching the land with legumes, to be plowed under while green, the bacteria on the roots of which gather nitrogen from the air, but you must add manure and/or make compost to maintain the fertility.

One ton of ordinary stable manure contains about 1275 pounds of organic matter, carrying eight pounds of nitrogen, ten pounds of potash, and four pounds of phosphoric acid.

Land must be well drained, it must contain a sufficient amount of humus, or decaying vegetable matter, to make it loose and porous; it must be free from sticks and stones or any foreign matter likely to impede cultivation or obstruct growth. The proper formation of a seed bed is a prime prerequisite to successful cropping. After the land is manured and plowed it should be gone over in all directions with a disk and smoothing harrow, until it is of a dustlike fineness.

Hotbeds

To get an early start on the garden or for raising plants for field crops, a hotbed is all but indispensable. Hot beds are right-angled boxes covered with glass panes set in movable frames and placed over heated excavations. The bed may be of any size or shape, but the standard one is six feet wide, since the stock glass frames are usually six feet long by three feet wide. The bed ought to face south or southeast and be well protected on the north. It should be banked all around with earth or straw to keep out the cold, and mats or shutters should be provided for extra cold weather. The best material for heating the bed and the most easily obtained, is fresh horse manure in which there is a quantity of straw or litter. This will give out a slow, moist heat and will not burn out before the crops or the plants mature.

Before sowing any seeds put a thermometer in the bed three inches deep in the soil. If it runs over 80 degrees Fahrenheit, do not sow, rather mix in more soil. If below 55 degrees it is too cold; you will have to fork it over and add more manure.

One eighth acre in early cauliflower and cabbage, about 2000 plants, if transplanted, would require two 6 x 12 frames, from 200 to 250 plants being grown under each sash. These frames may be used again for tomato plants for the same area, using about 450 plants. This will allow a sash for every 55 plants.

One frame should be in use at the same time for egg-plants and peppers, two sashes of each, growing 50 trans-planted plants under each sash. Two frames will be required for cucumbers, melons, and early squashes; for extra early lettuce, an estimate of 60 to 70 heads should be made to a sash. Celery, carrots and late cabbages can be started in seed beds in the open.

Greenhouses

Some kind of a greenhouse is necessary, but most are greatly overpriced for marginal gains in performance. The ideal greenhouse is one in which the light is most nearly that which exists outside, and in which the heat is as evenly distributed. It is practical experience that a structure with as

---

Spicy Cabbage Salad
6 to 8 servings

8 cups shredded cabbage (about 1/2 head)
1 medium onion, thinly sliced
1 large carrot, shredded
1 Tablespoon canola oil
1 teaspoon salt
1/2 teaspoon powdered ginger
1 teaspoon tumeric
2 Tablespoons peanut butter
2 Tablespoons water
1 teaspoon sugar
1/4 teaspoon crushed red pepper flakes
Heat a big skillet, add oil and onion and fry 2 minutes. Add cabbage and salt, fry about 10 minutes, until it softens. Mix spices, peanut butter, water and sugar, pour over vegetables, cook 2 minutes. Stir in carrot, mix well.

Easy Coleslaw
6 servings

1/2 head green cabbage (about 5 cups), shredded
1/2 cup white vinegar
1/3 cup sugar
1/2 teaspoon salt
1/2 cup evaporated milk
Pour vinegar over cabbage. Sprinkle on sugar and salt. Pour milk over and let stand 20-30 minutes. Be sure to follow this order so dressing doesn't curdle. Mix well and chill 2 hours.

Pineapple Coleslaw

Add one 7 oz. can crushed pineapple to coleslaw.

---

few angles and turns as possible and with a minimum of woodwork best answers these conditions.

Heating of greenhouses is best done by hot water, and we have found that a wood-fired hot-tub makes a splendid addition to our winter greenhouse. If you are willing to take a hot bath on every cold night, no independent heating plant is necessary. Hot water can be left to slowly dissipate its heat to the air or sent by pipes to warm and irrigate the beds.

Mushrooms

Many fungi are poisonous, so don't pick any you are not absolutely certain of. Easy to identify varieties include the boletes, chanterelles, oyster, and sulphur shelf, which are tasty and nutritious. Fungi dry very readily. Dried mushrooms can be added to soup and stews or soaked in water for several hours to regain texture.

Many people are afraid to pick wild mushrooms because of early childhood associations of mushrooms as poison. When you cultivate particular mushrooms however, you know what to expect and are not likely to confuse what comes up with something else that is not good for you.

Easy-to-Identify

Morels are distinctive in their variegated black or brown cap and white stem. Chanterelles, golden-orange and prized for their apricot flavor, are distinguished by a trumpet-like flare of white gills which is uninterrupted out to the edge of the cap. Giant puffballs are easily distinguished by their size, but if in doubt, slice open and look for vestigal cap formation, something a puffball would never have.

Growing Shiitake

Perhaps one of the best sources of protein which you can grow at home is the shiitake mushroom. It contains more digestible nutritional value, pound for pound, than meat, milk, eggs, cheese, or soybeans.

Shiitake, with its cracked, fleshy top—deep brown in the center and lightly misted with white flecks at the edges—is difficult to confuse with other oak-dwelling mushrooms.

In the sixties, many consumers became more concerned about their health, and, at about the same time, the medical research on shiitake's phenomenal benefits began coming in. Today those benefits are well-documented. Shiitake contains a high-potency mix of amino acids and strong immune-boosting interleukin compounds. Shiitake's powerful immune-boosting action reverses the T-cell suppression caused by tumors, making it a valuable ally against cancer, leukemia, lymphosarcoma and Hodgkin's disease. Antiviral actions, due to substances present in spores and mycelia, inhibit cell division of viruses, impeding the spread of flus and other infections. One shiitake mushroom, cooked in a tablespoon of butter, actually reduces serum cholesterol. In Japan it is taken to prevent heart disease because it regulates both high and low blood pressure. As an antiinflammatory, it improves stomach and duodenal ulcers, neuralgia, gout, constipation and hemorrhoids. Shiitake also counteracts fatigue, generates stamina and improves the complexion.

One of the choicest, most flavorful mushrooms, shiitake is also one of the easiest to grow at home. Complete kits to keep a home kitchen supplied year-round can be purchased for $20 from Mushroom*people*, PO Box 220, Summertown TN 38483, (931) 964-2200, www.thefarm.org/mushroom/.

Sprouts

Sprouts will provide you with fresh, nutritious food. You will need:

- a wide-mouth jar with mesh top (made from a window screen or cheesecloth)
- shade and warmth (closet, cupboard)

Remember, the larger the seed, the longer the soak. Rinse water can be used in cooking. The process is:

1. Cover seeds with water, rinse several times.

2. Cover with water, soak overnight.

3. Drain, rinse, keep jar inverted at an angle. Rinse several times a day until sprouts form. Spread on a towel to dry before using as salad or in stir-fry or sandwiches.

Seed	Days	Amt for 1 Qt	Green on Last Day?
Alfalfa	4 to 6	2 Tablespoons	yes
Lentil	3 to 5	1/2 cup	no
Mung*	3 to 5	1/3 cup	no
*soak for 20 hours			

Pasta with Mushroom Sauce

4 servings

1 ounce dried mushrooms, stems removed
2 cups boiling water (save after straining)
1 onion, chopped
1 teaspoon salt
2 cloves garlic, minced
1 Tablespoon olive oil
4 ounces tomato paste
1 teaspoon each dried basil and oregano
8 oz angel hair pasta, cooked, drained

Pour boiling water over mushrooms, let stand 1 hour. Remove mushrooms and chop, strain liquid through a piece of cheesecloth or thin towel to catch any grit and save liquid to add to sauce. Heat a skillet, add oil and onion and fry a few minutes. Add salt and chopped mushrooms, cook 10 to 15 minutes. Stir in tomato paste, reserved liquid, basil and oregano. Simmer and stir. Cook pasta, drain. Toss with sauce.

Shiitake Joes

6 servings

1 cup TVP
7/8 cup hot water
1 Tablespoon soy sauce
1 teaspoon dehydrated onion
6 rehydrated shiitake mushrooms, diced
1 Tablespoon canola oil
1 15 oz. can tomatoes with peppers
2 teaspoons chili powder

Pour hot water over TVP and let stand 10 minutes. Stir in soy sauce and onion. Heat a pan, add oil, add TVP and mushrooms and lightly brown. Stir in chili and tomatoes. Heat and serve over rice or biscuits.

"Since our emergence as a species, human populations have continually run up against local environmental limits: the inability to find sufficient game, grow enough food, or harvest enough wood has led to sudden collapses in human numbers and in some cases to the disappearance of entire civilizations. Although it may seem that advancing technology and the emergence of an integrated world economy have ended this age-old pattern, they may have simply transferred the problem to the global level."

—Lester R. Brown and Christopher Flavin, *State of the World 1999*

"The word impossible is not in my dictionary."

—Napolean Bonaparte

"There's no point in sugarcoating the problem. If we don't fix the century-date problem, we will have a situation scarier than the average disaster movie you might see on a Sunday night."

—Dr. Edward Yardeni

Afterword

In the ancient story, Icarus was the young scientist who learned to fly from watching the movements of birds. His artificial wings carried him high into the sky until the heat of the sun melted the wax that held the feathers to his arms. He suffered, to use the terms of the nuclear power industry, a "catastrophic disassembly."

The ancient story was about hubris, and the moral is that we should never leave the tendencies of nature too far removed from our planning. Failing to observe the constraints of gravity, sunlight, and the frailty of material things, Icarus was certain to fall.

Today our world has begun to resemble something out of The Jetsons. Ancient pharaohs could not conceive of the wealth and power that the average Westerner now takes for granted. But beneath the surface, our hubris is all too evident.

Nature has always sustained us. We inhabit a thin film of biological activity in the cold depths of space, many light years from any other star system. No other planet in our own solar system is hospitable to life. Our own planet's biosphere is thinner, by proportion, than the dew on an apple. We are one large solar flare, one errant asteroid, or one nuclear winter away from extinction.

Looking around, we should be amazed and reverential that we have been given paradise for the span of a lifetime. Instead, we are collectively polluting, overconsuming, and wasting it to death. By any reasonable index—diversity of species, soil productivity, fresh water, forest cover, carbon in the atmosphere, ozone over the poles—we are squandering our inheritance at unprecedented rates. We are doubtless well beyond carrying capacity already: if everyone now alive consumed at a North American standard it would take 3 planets this size to provide the daily menu. Even that would last less than 20 years before a 4th planet were needed. World population, which has already doubled twice in our lifetimes, is headed for 11 billion in the next century, even if fertility were to be held to sum zero: 1.4 births per couple. Half a child more, and we push at 18 billion. Half a child less, and we stay where we are.

Wait a minute. Half a child less and we stay where we are?

That means there is still something we can do. We might even be able to reverse our disastrous march toward global suicide and "get back to the garden." We know how. It is no mystery. You take care of the soil, and the water. You stop burning fossil fuels and look to the sun for heat and light. You move towards egalitarian, healthy, humane systems of social development. You take care of nature.

Y2K may be the trigger for a global economic depression that lasts for many years. Or it may not. It may plunge us into violent anarchy and military rule. Or it may not. But if Y2K doesn't wake us up to the precariousness of our condition, divorced from our roots in the soil and the forest, annihilating the evolutionary systems that sustain us and replacing them with brittle, artificial, plastic imitations, what will? What will it take?

Y2K is an opportunity to pause, to think through our present course, and to adjust to a saner path for the future.

Those of us who have been working with sustainable development issues in the past century see this as a great opportunity for public education and activism. In the ecovillage movement, which is about redesigning human settlements, we see Y2K as a recruitment bonanza, driving millions of people to suddenly want to learn about making communities more regenerative, resilient, and self-sufficient.

Organic gardeners, permaculturists, homesteaders, small farmers, silvaculturists and aquaculturists all stand to benefit. Healers, herbalists, natural builders, solar engineers, seed catalogs—anyone who was on the sustainability track to begin with is poised to take a big step forward.

Y2K is a horrible predicament. It is also a wonderful opportunity to do a lot better. Let's not squander the moment.

"More than one-third of the most important [government] systems won't be fixed in time."

—House Panel Y2K report, September 1998

"We're concerned about the potential disruption of power grids, telecommunications and banking services."

Sherry Burns, CIA, 1998

Shopping Lists and Sources

Albert and Dorothy have very different shopping lists. As their houses and cooking equipment differ, so will the foods they stockpile. Both lists include an assortment of jams, jellies, pickles, ketchup, mustards, various herb teas, instant coffee, grains and flour, dried milk, dried TVP, several pounds of Good Tasting Nutritional Yeast (1-800-695-2241) and seeds suitable for sprouting.

Albert plans to feed a large number of drop-ins for 3 months or longer, and to supplement his stored food with fresh garden produce including fresh winter greens from his strawbale greenhouse. He has gas and wood ranges and a volcano stove and plans to have a large supply of both propane and firewood on hand. His house has a wood burning furnace and he stores water from his roof in a 500-gallon cistern. He plans to have enough water so he can wash and soak dried beans. He also grows and dries a large supply of shiitake mushrooms, culinary herbs, and chile peppers each summer.

ALBERT'S LIST:

50 pounds soybeans	25 pounds 10-bean mix
50 pounds TVP, all flavors	25 pounds black beans
50 pounds hard red wheat	25 pounds dried kidney beans
50 pounds all-purpose flour	25 pounds dried lentils
50 pounds sugar	25 pounds popcorn
50 pounds whole yellow corn	3 pounds garbanzo beans
25 pounds cornmeal	3 pounds green split peas
25 pounds white enriched rice	3 containers of baking soda
25 pounds white enriched flour	1 large container baking
25 pounds dried pinto beans	powder

The Y2K Survival Guide

1 pound baking yeast
5 pounds nutritional yeast
5 pounds salt
5 gallons vinegar
25 pounds instant dry milk
50 pounds (5 gal) honey
25 pounds long white rice
25 pounds brown rice
40 pounds potato flakes
30 pounds onions
30 pounds raisins

25 pounds rolled oatmeal
20 pounds pasta noodles, spaghetti, etc.
5 gallons olive oil
2 gallons canola oil
1 gallon soy sauce
5 pounds nut butters
20 pounds butter
Bay leaves and spices
Canned fruits and vegetables

Dorothy plans to use her fireplace for cooking plus a chafing dish and possibly a two-burner camp stove with folding oven. She will rely on canned foods to a large extent to conserve water. With no basement or attic, her storage space is limited.

DOROTHY'S LIST:

Beans:

6 cans each of chili beans, pinto beans, black beans, red kidney beans, cannellini beans, garbanzo beans.
6 packages of lentils, 2 packages of split peas.

Grains:

25 pounds enriched white rice, including some instant rice and boil-in-a-bag rice. 25 pounds white enriched flour.

Several packages of couscous, angel hair pasta, thin spaghetti, bow ties, orzo, buckwheat groats (kasha), rice noodles. (About 25 pounds in all). Buy 2 boxes of Hummus, too.

Packages of: Textured Vegetable Protein granules, good tasting Nutritional Yeast (The Mail Order Catalog)

Fruits:

6 cans each of grapefruit, peaches, pears, plums, apricots, pineapple. Also several packages of dried fruit: apples, apricots, bananas, raisins, pineapple, prunes.

Juices:

6 cans/bottles each apple, cranberry, grapefruit, grape and tomato juice.

Vegetables:

12 cans whole peeled tomatoes, 6 cans tomato sauce, 6 cans tomato paste, 12 cans sweet potatoes, 4 cans beets, 2 jars red cabbage, 3 jars marinated artichoke hearts, 3 cans asparagus tips, 6 jars roasted red peppers or pimentos, 6 cans green beans, 6 cans corn, both whole kernel and cream style, 6 cans green chilies, and several boxes of Instant Mashed Potatoes. Also dried tomatoes.

Staples:

20 pounds white sugar, 5 pounds brown sugar, 1 gallon olive oil, 2 gallons canola oil, 2 gallons vinegar, bouillon cubes, dried onion soup mix, chutney, packaged parmesan cheese, cocoa, instant coffee, tea.

Goodie Foods:

Several bags of pretzels, low fat tostito chips, a dozen boxes of cookies, low fat potato chips, root beer and diet sodas.

Spices:

Bay leaves, allspice, basil, cayenne, chili powder, cumin, coriander, cinnamon, curry powder, dill, garlic powder, onion powder, dehyrated onion, dried parsley, marjoram, nutmeg, oregano, paprika, dried red pepper flakes, sage, thyme, tumeric. Good Tasting Nutritional Yeast has most essential vitamins and adds terrific flavor to virtually any dish—an all-purpose spice!

Don't forget bleach, toilet paper, and vitamin pills!

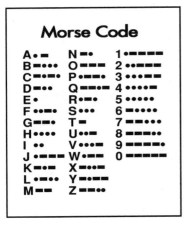

Kasha and Bow Ties

3 Tablespoons oil, divided
1 cup kasha (toasted buckwheat groats)
2 cups boiling hot water
1 large onion, chopped
8 ounces bow tie pasta, cooked

Heat Dutch oven or heavy pan. Add 1 tablespoon oil, kasha and hot water. Cover and cook about 15 minutes. Fry onion in 2 Tablespoons oil, add to kasha. Toss grains with cooked pasta.

Tabouli   4 servings

1 cup bulgur wheat
1 1/2 cup water
1/2 teaspoon salt
1 carrot, grated
2 teaspoons dried mint leaves
2 whole (canned) tomatoes, chopped
2 Tablespoons chopped onion
1/4 cup lemon juice
1/4 cup olive oil
1 Tablespoon dried parsley

Bring the water to a boil, add the salt and pour over the wheat in a ceramic or glass bowl. Stir, cover and let stand 1 hour or more. Add the carrot, mint leaves, tomatoes and onion. Mix the lemon juice and olive oil, stir into wheat and vegetables. Sprinkle with dried parsley to garnish.

Shopping Lists

Here are some specific collectables of the types we've mentioned, and some of the better prices currently available:

Supplier	Item Desc.	Price
Clothes		
Cheaper Than Dirt	Swiss wool jacket	$9.97
Sportsmans Guide	Rugged barn coat	$17.97
Sportsmans Guide	Navy bell-bottom wool pants	$14.97
Sportsmans Guide	Brush overpants	$9.97
Sportsmans Guide	French expandable field pants	$7.97

Sportsmans Guide	Austrian coveralls	$14.97
Sportsmans Guide	Military pants liner	$7.97
Sportsmans Guide	Italian police coat	$14.97
Sportsmans Guide	Belgian military coat	$16.97
Sportsmans Guide	Wool pants	$12.97
Sportsmans Guide	French canvas raincoat	$9.97
Sportsmans Guide	Dutch 4-pocket work pants	$14.97
Sportsmans Guide	Swiss wool bacalavas	$4.97

Food

Revelation	72-hour traveler pack	$154.00
Revelation	One-month emergency unit	$215.00
Revelation	3-month Pantry	$389.00
Walton Feed	One year deluxe food storage unit	$947.00
Walton Feed	Butter powder	$18.15
The Mail Order Co.	Nutritional Yeast, TVP	from $20.00
Herbal Advantage	Stevia extract (non-spoiling sweetener)	$81.00
Watertanks	Square plastic pail	$4.95

Garden

Lehmans	Non-hybrid seed assortment	$19.95
Ark	Non-hybrid seeds	$159.00
Mushroompeople	Shiitake Starter Kit	$19.95
Lehmanns	Rotary cultivator	$115.00
Sportsmans Guide	Machete	$5.97
Lehmanns	Reel mower	$225.00
Lehmanns	Scythe blade	$57.95
Lehmanns	Scythe handle	$67.95
Lehmanns	Fiberglass-handle wood axe	$35.00
Cheaper Than Dirt	Pocket saw	$6.97
Cheaper Than Dirt	Leatherman Wave Tool	$79.97
Cheaper Than Dirt	Folding shovel	$5.97

Heat

Lehmanns	Wood-burning stoves	prices from $199
Lehmanns	Leather hand bellows	$34.95
Lehmanns	Barrel stove kit	$79.00
Lehmanns	Mounting kit for smoke chamber	$29.95
Northern Hydraulics	Portable propane heater	$86.99
Northern Hydraulics	11,000-btu propane heater	$49.99
Campmor	Space Blanket	$3.25
Campmor	Survival Blanket	$10.00
Campmor	Magnesium firestarting tool	$5.00
Campmor	25 Storm matches	$4.00

Household

Lehmanns	Non-electric shaver	$45.00
Lehmanns	Balance beam measuring scale	$99.00
Lehmanns	Clothes washboard	$17.95
Cheaper Than Dirt	Gray polyester blankets	$5.97
Sportsmans Guide	German sewing kit	$3.97
Cheaper Than Dirt	Straight razor	$19.97

Kitchen

| Northern Hydraulics | Single-burner propane stove | $34.99 |

Rocky Mtn Volcano	Large Dutch Oven	$89.00
Rocky Mtn Volcano	Volcano Stove	$99.00
Cheaper Than Dirt	Single burner propane stove	$15.97
Cheaper Than Dirt	Camping cookware	$5.97
Cheaper Than Dirt	Can openers	$1.97
Lehmanns	Wood cookstoves	prices from $199.00
Lehmanns	Dough kneader	$49.95
Lehmanns	Cheese slicer	$19.95
Lehmanns	Non-electric food processor	$99.00
Lehmanns	Clamp-on meat grinder	$39.00
Lehmanns	Butter churn	$199.00
Lehmanns	Apple peeler/corer/slicer	$39.95
Lehmanns	Hanging food dryer	$39.95
Lehmanns	Canner	$19.95
Lehmanns	Juicer	$57.00
Lehmanns	Country living grain mill	$359.00
Lehmanns	Noodle maker	$45.00
Lehmanns	Knife sharpener	$9.95
Lehmanns	Clay water cooler	$49.95
Lehmanns	Coffee Mill	$95.00
Lehmanns	Cheese press	$219.00
Lehmanns	Grain mill	$149.00
Lehmanns	Stainless steel funnel	$12.95
Lehmanns	All in one kitchen tool	$4.85
Lehmanns	Instant apple slicer	$3.00
Lehmanns	Egg beater	$38.00
Lehmanns	Rolling pin	$19.95
Lehmanns	Vegetable peeler	$5.25
Lehmanns	Apple corer	$10.95
Lehmanns	Flour sifter	$23.95
Lehmanns	Vegetable slicer	$7.95
Sportsmans Guide	Utensil set	$4.97

Light

Northern Hydraulics	Solar-powered flashlight	$9.99
Cheaper Than Dirt	12 yellow 12-hour light sticks	$0.99
Cheaper Than Dirt	High-powered flashlight	$62.99
RealGoods	White LED flashlight	$18.95
RealGoods	Hand-powered flashlight	$56.95
Lehmanns	Dietz Blizzard lanterns	$18.95
Lehmanns	Wicks for Dietz lanterns	$0.50
Lehmanns	Burners for Dietz lanterns	$6.95
Watertanks	100 100-hr candles	$24.95

Medical

Herbal Advantage	Grapefruit seed extract	$19.65
Sportsmans Guide	Military medical kit	$34.97
Masune	100 Iodine prep pads	$5.65
Masune	100 Betadine swab pads	$6.65
Masune	12 antiseptic towelettes	$2.95
WalMart	Isopropyl alcohol	$12.50
WalMart	100 alcohol prep pads	$1.75
WalMart	Hydrogen peroxide	$1.05
Masune	75 Antibiotic ointment packets	$16.25
Masune	Anbesol gel oral (dental anesthesic)	$16.80
Masune	Sterile gauze pads	$17.05
Masune	Cotton balls (500)	$17.05

Masune	Activated charcoal	$8.80
Masune	4" x 5 yd. elastic bandages	$2.25
Cheaper Than Dirt	12-pack of gauze rolls	$3.45
Cheaper Than Dirt	Surgical suture kit	$3.97

Tools

Shomer-Tec/ Campmor	Watchband compass	$8.95
Cheaper Than Dirt	Survival hatchet	$5.97
Cheaper Than Dirt	Bushman knife	$12.97
Cheaper Than Dirt	Rescue knife	$5.97
Cheaper Than Dirt	Sleeping bags (used)	$34.97
Cheaper Than Dirt	Binoculars	$24.97
Lehmanns	Hand-powered drill	$65.95
Cheaper Than Dirt	Fishing rod	$19.97
Cheaper Than Dirt	368-Pc. Fishing tackle	$69.97
Cheaper Than Dirt	Pkg. of 5 lip balm	$1.97
Cheaper Than Dirt	Survival techniques CD-ROM	$14.97
Cheaper Than Dirt	Hand-powered AM radio and light	$19.97
RealGoods	Hand-powered or solar radio	$56.95
Sportsmans Guide	Battery shortwave radio	$49.97
Radioland	Hand-crank Bay-Gen radio	$99.00
Alternative Energy	Solar Charger for Bay-Gen radio	$26.00
Northern Hydraulics	Hand-crank shortwave radio	$59.97
Northern Hydraulics	Hand-crank AM-FM radio	$72.99
Sportsmans Guide	Swedish helmet liner	$7.97
Sportsmans Guide	Swedish steel helmet	$9.97
Cheaper Than Dirt	Sewing awl	$7.97

Water

Watertanks	55-gal blue plastic drum	$38.95
Watertanks	Barrel pump (55 gal)	$24.95
Northern Hydraulics	Barrel pump (55 gal)	$16.99
Northern Hydraulics	Drum pump (15 gal)	$12.99
Northern Hydraulics	Cast-iron hand pump (23' depth)	$57.99
Walmart	30-gal plastic trash cans	$8.00
Lehmanns, Campmor	Katadyn water filter	$249.00
Sportsmans Guide	Pour-through filter	$4.97
Watertanks	1050-gal water bag	$298.95
Watertanks	200-gal water bag	$88.95
Watertanks	220-gal waterbox	$188.95
Watertanks	55-gal plastic drum	$48.95
Watertanks	Barrel pump (55 gal)	$24.95
Freund	Small closed head plastic drums	$8.51
Cheaper Than Dirt	British water jug	$12.97

For computer users: making the world seem normal after Y2k

- Use a doubleclick to turn on the lights in your rooms
- Place bookmarks at favorite places in your home
- Start newsgroups on the bulletin board atyour store
- Pick up old things from your trash that you regret you had thrown away
- Put up an hourglass when you work very hard
- Decorate your walls with a desktop pattern
- If anything goes wrong during the day, reboot... go back to bed and start all over again.

SOURCES

Bulk Foods

Alpineaire Foods: 800-322-6325, Sales@Alpineairefoods.com, www.alpineairefoods.com/

American Harvest Foods: 800-500-3858

B&A Products: www.baproducts.com

Back To Basics: basics@dnet.net, www.dnet.net/~Basics/

Best Prices Stored Food: 972-288-0262, foodstr2@airmail.net, web2.airmail.net/foodstr2/

Bronson's Pharmaceutical: : 800-235-3200

CSIN: 512-478-4922, castig@flash.net

Emergency Essentials: 800-999-1863, askeei@beprepared.com, www.beprepared.com/Home.html/

Freeze Dry Foods: Info@freeze-dry.com, www.freeze-dry.com/

Happy Hovel Foods: 800-637-7772, haphov@seanet.com, www.wwmagic.com/Haphov/

Harvest Foodworks: 800-268-4268, thefolks@harvest.on.ca, www.harvest.on.ca

Homestead Foods: 800-838-3132

Lakeridge Food Storage: 800-336-7127, lfsfood@Ix.netcom.com, www.shopsite.com/Lfs/

Live Oak Farms: 888-359-5596, ron@universalweb.com, www.universalweb.com/Food/

Major Surplus: 800-441-8855

Maple Leaf Industries, Inc.: 800-671-5323, food@mapleleafinc.com, www.mapleleafinc.com/

Meyers Custom Supply: 800-451-6105, mcs@c-zone.net, www.c-zone.net/meyerscs/mcs/

Nitro-pak Preparedness Center: 800-866-487, 888-648-7672, Nitropak@Shadowlink.net, www.nitro-pak.com

Oregon Freeze Dry: 800-547-0244, mtnhouse@ofd.com, www.ofd.com/Mh/

Perma-Guard (Diatomaceous Earth): 505-873-3061

Product Source International: psiusa@aros.net, www.downtown-web.com/Psi/

Ready Reserve Foods: 800-453-2202:

Sam Andy Foods: 800-331-0358:

Sopakco: 800-776-8731, Mlbailey@Worldnet.att.net, www.sopakco.com:

Star Food Processing, Inc.: 800-882-meal

Vitamin Shoppe: 800-223-1216

Walton Feed, Inc.: 800-269-8563, mark@waltonfeed.com, waltonfeed.com

Tools

American Freedom Network: 800-205-6245 Orders@Amerifree.com, www.amerifree.com/Index.htm

Berlin Packaging: 800-423-7546, Info@berlinpackaging.com, www.berlinpackaging.com

Brigade Quartermasters: 800-338-4327

Campmor: 800-226-7667, Info@campmor.com, www.campmor.com

Cheaper Than Dirt: Tel: 888-625-3848, Fax: 800-596-5655

Con Yeager Spice Company: 800-222-2460, Bkrever@Fyi.net, www.nauticom.net/W-pa/Yeager.htm

Consolidated Plastics: 800-362-1000

Cumberland General Store: 800-334-4640

Double Springs Homebrew Supply: 888-499-2739, Homebrew@Goldrush.com, www.doublesprings.com/

Drumco: 501-557-5500 901-396-6484, Fax: 501-557-5574, 901-398-0987

Energy Outfitters Ltd.: 800-GO-SOLAR (467-6527), www.energyoutfitters.com/catalog.htm

Freund hard-to-find containers: 773/224-4230, Ext. 179

Glitchproof: www.glitchproof.com

Golden Genesis: 800-544-6466, www.goldengenesis.com

Harbor Freight: 800-423-2567, www.harborfreight.com

Home Canning Supply & Specialties: 800-354-4070

Jade Mountain: 303-449-6601

Koch Supplies: 800-456-5624, Koch@Kochsupplies.com, www.kochsupplies.com

Lehmann's Non-Electric Catalog: 330-857-5757, fax: 330-857-5785, getinfo@lehmans.com, www.lehmans.com:

Life Sprouts: 800-241-1516

Masune: 800-831-0894, Fax: 800-222-1934:

Nasco: 800-558-9595,
www.nascoofa.com
Northern Hydraulics: 800-533-5545
Penzeys, Ltd. Spice House:
Info@penzeys.com,
www.penzeys.com
Real Goods Company: 800-762-7325
Revelation Arms: 503-642-9066,
503-642-1868,
revelat@hevanet.com
Shomer-Tec: Tel: 360-733-6214 Fax:
360-676-5248
Sportsman's Guide: 800-882-2962
Survival Books: 818-704-1818, Fax
818-704-0322
United States Plastics: 800-537-
9724, usp@usplastics.com,
www.usplastic.com

Heirloom Seeds: PO Box 245, W.
Elizabeth PA 15088-0245
Herbal Advantage: Tel: 918-386-
2654; Fax: 918-386-2933
Horizon Herbs: 541-846-6704,
herbseed@chatlink.com
Johnny's Seeds: 207-437-9294, fax:
800-437-4290,
www.johnnyseeds.com
Mushroom*people:* 800-FUNGI-96,
mushroom@thefarm.org,
www,thefarm.org/mushroom
Park Seed: 800-845-3366,
wholesale@parkseed.com
Ronniger's Seed Potatoes: Star
Route, Moyie Springs, ID 83845
Seeds of Change Organic Seeds:
505-438-0821

Grasshopper Quesadillas — Serves 6

About 1000 grasshoppers (the younger the better)
1/2 cup chili sauce
pinch of salt
garlic
onion
1 lemon
1 cup guacamole
6 tortillas

Soak the grasshoppers in clean water for 24 hours. Boil them, then let dry. Fry in a pan with garlic, onion, salt and lemon. Roll up in tortillas with chili sauce and guacamole.

Volcano Stoves: 800-454-1995,
www.rmvolcano.com
Watertanks: 888-742-6275 or 760-
727-3266
Wornick Company: 800-565-4147,
www.wornick.com

Seeds
Abundant Life Seed Foundation: 360-
385-5660
The Ark Institute: 800-255-1912
Bethlehem Seed Company: 610-954-
5443
Burpee Heirloom Catalog: 800-888-
1447
Down on the Farm Seed: PO Box
184, Hiram, OH 44234
Empire National Nursery:
nursery@cdr3.com,
www.cdr3.com/berry
Endangered/Heirloom Vegetable:
4N381-OG Maple Ave,
Bensenville, IL 60106
Forest Farm Nursery: 541-846-7269
Fox Hollow Herb & Heirloom Seed
Company: 724-548-7333
Gurneys Seed & Nursery Company:
605-665-9310

Territorial Seed Co.: 541-942-9547
The Pure Seed Co.: 604-774-1001,
william-e-
brown@compuserve.com
Wild Weeds: 707-786-4906

Y2K Internet Bookmarks

These sites were among the best as of February, 1999. We have these and newer links from our own site at y2k@ecovillage. org. Any http://www prefixes have been omitted.

4link.net/~pluto/y2k.html
akinet.com/year2000/
all-systems.com
anamorph.com/y2k.html
angelfire.com/ak2/y2kprep
angelfire.com/mn/plan4y2k
ans2000.com
auditserve.com/yr2000/yr2ksem.html
c2isolutions.com
cassandraproject.org
christiany2k.com
cinderella.co.za
cnet.com/Content/Reports/Special/Y2K
cnnfn.com/digitaljam/newsbytes
co-intelligence.org

comlinks.com
context.org
coolandunusual.com/y2k/y2kstore
cruxnet.com/~sanger/y2k/
csf.colorado.edu/sustainability
csis.org/html/y2k.html
cy2kr.com
disasterrelief.org/Library/Prepare
dispatches.azstarnet.com/Y2K/read.htm
doi.gov/oirm/y2k/y2kpage2.html
doit.state.ct.us/y2k/humor.htm
eljay.holyoak.com
emeraldcoast.com/~perpetual/Y2K.htm
EmpowermentResources.com
euy2k.com
familysupplies.com/1-y2k-preparedness
fdn.net/y2k
fema.gov/pte/prep2.htm
ffiec.gov/y2k
firstgalaxy.com/2000fix
fnb.co.za/y2k
foodbanking.com
foodbanking.com/food1.htm
foodbanking.freeservers.com
foodstorageonline.com
foody2k.freeservers.com
forscom.army.mil/y2k/armylink.htm
friend.ly.net/GEET/backup.htm
gaia.org
gao.gov/y2kr.htm
garynorth.com
geocities.com/PicketFence/3949/
global-merchants.com/home/y2k.htm
gracenet.com/Y2K
gracenet.com/y2k
headland.com/y2k
holyoak.com/y2k
holyoak.com/y2kdisc
home.swbell.net/adheath/testimony.htm
house.gov/reform/gmit/y2k
hp.com/year2000/products.html
ic.org
icehouse.net/cornerstone/y2k.htm
icl.com/year2000
ineedhelpnow.com
infogoal.com/cbd/cbdy2k.htm
insightdiscounts.com/
      y2k_preparedness.htm
investpacific.com
iso-ne.com/y2k_statement
istinfo.com
itpolicy.gsa.gov/mks/yr2000
jademountain.com
jps.net/tlcserv/1.htm
jvprofit.com/jrdir/y2k.htm
kenraggio.com/KRPNSurvivalTactics.htm
kiyoinc.com/current.html
lanovation.com
leonardsloan.com/about/y2k/
      y2ktshirts.htm
lifelink.com/statelst.htm
lightlink.com/y2k
lightlink.com/y2k
lincoln.midcoast.com/~jpfisher/
      lcy2kpc.htm
living-foods.com/articles
lookup.org/EmergencyFood.htm
lowcostliving.com
lowellonline.org/bna/y2k/
mcalvany.com
members.xoom.com/esada/
millenniumtools.com/free/cure12.htm
mitre.org/research/y2k/docs/
      CONTINGENCY_GUIDELINES.html
mitre.org/research/y2k/docs/PROB.html

nasire.org/year2000/coordinators.html
nccn.net/~wwithin/wncy2k.htm
neolith.com
news.com/News/Item
newsbureau.com/archives/aug97/
      scotsystems.htm
noahspantry.com
nonviolence.org/tranet
oecd.org/puma/gvrnance/it/y2k.htm
open.org/memanage/y2k/y2k.htm
parsifal.membrane.com/y2k/
partsonsale.com/y2kelecprepare.html
personal.pitnet.net/kramlow/y2k/
preparednessmart.com
pti.nw.dc.us/membership/y2k/
readyfory2k.com
redcross.org/disaster/safety/y2k.html
rharris.com
romtran.com
rv-y2k.org
sailnet.msfc.nasa.gov:8001/y2k_home
sba.gov/y2k
scp.hqisec.army.mil/y2kresults.html
securenet.org
senate.gov/~bennett/y2k.html
senate.gov/~y2k
sightings.com/ufo/y2kdatapage.html
silkmoth.com/download/y2k.htm
solstice.crest.org
spil-india.com/
sportssolutionsinc.com
state.wy.us/ai/itd/y2000
successinformation.com/game.htm
supplies4y2k.com
support2000.com
techweb.com
they2ksite.com
tmn.com/y2k
tqminc.com/data_commander.htm
transcend2000.com
treehouse.com/y2k.html
tvsonline.net/~alberts/prepare
unitedway.org/year2000
unix.cc.wmich.edu/rea/Y2K/FAQ.html
users.inna.net/~ymmarket/y2k.htm
users.itsnet.com/~foodnow/wwwboard/
      wwwboard.htm
utne.com
videohandbook.com
viscom.byu.edu/y2k
visitusa.com/oregon/y2k
visualsoft-usa.com/newhomepg/main/
      infocen.htm
w3.gorge.net/allied/y2kprep.htm
washington-online.com
westsound.com/ptmudge/y2k.htm
wilsonwhite.co.nz/y2k.htm
y2k-status.org/TelcomProblems.htm
y2k.co.uk/ceorca.htm
y2k.com
y2k.comco.org
y2k.gov.my
y2k.or.id
y2kwomen.com
y2kactionday.com
y2kcommunity.org
y2kcool.com
y2kcrisis2000.com/news.html
y2kfood.com
y2khour.com
y2kinvestor.com/intro.html
y2kmall.net
y2knapa.com
y2knet.com
y2knews-global.com

y2knews-it.com
y2knews.com
y2knewswire.com/riskmatrix.htm
y2knonit.com
y2kregister.com.au
y2kstore.com
y2kstormwatch.com/ffl/cs.htm
y2ksupply.com
y2ktimebomb.com
y2ktoday.com
y2ktool.com
y2kwatch.com
yardeni.com/y2kbook.html
year2000.com
year2000center.com
yourdon.com

Sheet Bend Carrick Bend

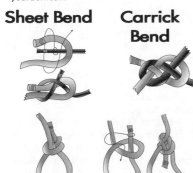

Slipknot Bowline

Permaculture is the science of designing sustainable culture. For information about permaculture philosophy, principles, and opportunities, visit www.thefarm.org/ permaculture/. See too www.ecovillage.org and www.ic.org for information on sustainable communities.

10-Codes

10-1 Receiving Poorly
10-2 Receiving Well
10-3 Stop Transmitting
10-4 OK, Message Received
10-5 Relay Message
10-6 Busy, Stand By
10-7 Out of Service, Leaving Air
10-8 In Service, Subject To Call
10-9 Repeat Message
10-10 Transmission Completed, Standing By
10-12 Visitors Present
10-13 Advise Weather
10-17 Urgent Business
10-18 Anything For Us?
10-19 Nothing For You, Return To Base
10-20 My Location Is___
10-21 Call By Landline
10-33 Emergency Traffic at this Station
10-34 Trouble At Ths Station, Help!
10-38 Ambulance Needed At___
10-44 I Have A Message For You
10-45 All Units Within Range Report
10-62 Unable To Copy, Use Landline
10-65 Waiting for Next Assignment
10-67 All Units Comply
10-70 Fire At_____
10-77 Negative Contact
10-93 Check My Frequency
10-99 Mission Completed, All Units Secure
10-100 5-Min. Break, Commonly Rest Room
10-200 Police Needed At____

Recommended Daily Allowances

Vitamin A	5,000 IU	Biotin	0.3 mg
Vitamin D	400 IU	Pantothenic Acid	10 mg
Vitamin E	10 IU	Calcium	1.0 g
Vitamin C	60 mg	Phosphorus	1.0 g
Folic Acid	0.4 mg	Iodine	150 mcg
Thiamin	1.5 mg	Iron	18 mg
Riboflavin	1.7 mg	Magnesium	400 mg
Niacin	20 mg	Copper	2.5 mg
Vitamin B6	2.0 mg	Zinc	15 mg
Vitamin B12	6.0 mcg	Protein	45 g

Trace: Selenium, Sodium, Chlorine, Potassium, Sulfur, Molybdenum, Cobalt, Fluorine, Boron, Chromium, Lithium, Nickel, Silicon, Tin, Vanadium, and Arsenic

WOUNDS

1. Control bleeding.
a. Apply direct pressure on wound with a sterile dressing (if available).
b. Elevate injured area above the heart if possible.
c. Apply pressure to supplying blood vessel if direct pressure is not successful.
2. Secure dry, sterile dressings with bandages.
3. Cleanse minor injuries thoroughly with plain soap and water (clean your hands first).
4. If evidence of infection appears, see a doctor.

FRAC-TURES

1. Do not move the victim.
2. Keep the broken bone ends and adjacent joints from moving.
3. If an open wound is present, control the bleeding (see wounds).
4. Apply splints.

SHOCK

1. Keep victim lying down.
2. Cover only enough to keep victim from losing body heat.
3. Obtain medical help as soon as possible.

IN CASE OF A SERI-OUS ACCIDENT:

1. RESCUE: Do not move victim unless further danger is imminent.
2. CHECK BREATHING: If not breathing, give artificial respiration.
3. CONTROL SEVERE BLEEDING: Use direct pressure and elevate.
4. DILUTE POISONS: With milk or water.
5. TREAT FOR SHOCK.
6. CALL FOR HELP.

POISONING

1. Dilute with milk or water (except for an unconscious person).
2. Call **POISON CONTROL CENTER 1-800-338-6167.**
3. If breathing stops, use artificial respiration.
4. Save label of poison container and/or save sample of vomitus.
5. Transport to hospital emergency room.

BURNS

1. To relieve pain and prevent contamination:
a. Submerge small minor burns in cold water (do not use ice).
b. Apply sterile dressings to large extensive burns (do not apply grease or ointment).
2. Treat for shock.
3. Seek medical assistance.
4. To alleviate pain for minor burns cover the area with the white juice of an aloe plant.

STOPPAGE OF BREATHING

1. Give artificial respiration - Mouth to mouth method:
a) Tip victim's head back, chin pointing up
b) Look, listen and feel for breathing
c) If not breathing, close victim's nostrils by pinching shut
d) Make a tight seal over victim's mouth with your mouth
e) Inflate victim's lungs with 2 full slow breaths
f) Watch victim's chest fall while listening for air return between breaths
g) Check for the pulse at the side of the neck for 5 seconds. If there is no pulse and there is no breathing, begin CPR if you have been trained.
h) If victim has a pulse, but is not breathing, give artificial respiration.
i) Breathe for adults once every 5 seconds; for

children, once every 4 seconds; for infants, once every 3 seconds.
j) Recheck for spontaneous breathing every few minutes.
2. Call an ambulance.

HEART ATTACK

Symptoms: Chest pains, difficulty breathing, nausea, sweating, weak rapid pulse. If you suspect a person has suffered a heart attack, search for an identification card or bracelet for additional steps or doctor's telephone number. Question eyewitnesses about what has occurred.
1. Place the victim in a comfortable position.
2. If victim is conscious, they should take one adult aspirin immediately.
3. Raise his head and chest if breathing is difficult.
4. If breathing stops, apply artificial respiration.
5. Get medical aid fast — physician or person trained in CPR.
6. If pulse becomes absent, give CPR if trained.

a. Tip head to open airway. Look, listen, feel for breathing.
b. Restore breathing. Give mouth-to-mouth artificial respiration.
c. Restore circulation. Check carotid pulse. If absent, apply external cardiac compression on the victim's breast bone.
Single Rescuer: 15 chest compressions at 80-100 per minute, alternate with 2 slow full lung inflations, then repeat 15 compressions.

Two Rescuers: 5 compressions at 90-100 per minute. Give 1 breath every 5th compression. Repeat at 5:1 ratio.

SIMPLE FAINTING

1. Keep victim lying down with feet elevated until recovery is complete.
2. Bathe face gently with cool water. Do not pour water over victim.
3. Loosen tight clothing. Keep crowds away.

HEAT EXHAUSTION

1. Provide rest, with feet elevated 8-12 inches.
2. Apply cool, wet cloths or rubbing alcohol to the victim.
3. Give sips of cool water, 1/2 glass every 15 minutes for 1 hour.
4. Loosen clothing.
5. Fan victim.
6. Victim should do no work for several days.

FROSTBITE

1. Protect the frozen area from further injury.
2. Cover the frozen area with clothing or blankets.
3. Do not rub frozen part since this may cause tissue death.
4. Immerse chilled part in warm water (102 - 108 degrees) as soon as possible.
5. If thawed and refrozen, immerse chilled part in room temperature water (70-74 degrees).
6. Do not use heat lamp, hot water bottle, or stove to warm the frostbitten area.
7. Discontinue warming the victim as soon as the affected part becomes flush.
8. If fingers or toes are involved, place dry sterile gauze between them to keep them separated.
9. If medical help is not available for 1 hour or more, give victim (conscious victims only) a weak solution of salt and soda at home or en route: 1 level teaspoon of salt and 1/2 level teaspoon of baking soda to each quart of water, neither hot or cold. Give about 4 ounces of 1/2 glass every 15 minutes (adults).
...take a Red Cross course

WATER RESCUE

You can help... even if you can't swim.

When a bather is in trouble near a dock, float, or side of pool, your number one priority is to stay on the dock.

1. Extend upper body over water, making sure you have a firm foothold.
2. Grasp victim's wrists.
3. Slowly draw victim to safety.

Or....

1. Extend a pole, towel, shirt, or branch to victim.
2. Draw victim to safety — don't let victim pull you into water!

Or....

Use buoy or other floatation device attached to rope. Stand one on end of rope, throw float beyond victim and slowly pull it into victim's grasp.

In a boat, on a beach, in shallow water...think first. Use oar or paddle... or a piece of wood.

Don't....

Let the victim pull you in over your head, or there may be two victims. Attempt a swimming rescue unless you are a trained lifesaver.

Nature Cures

Certain well-known weeds are sources of modern medicines. Roots, leaves, and flowers of several species considered weeds in the United States are gathered, cured, and used in other countries. The early American settlers learned from the Indians to use Golden Seal as a curative for sore and inflamed eyes, as well as for sore mouth. The plant grows in patches in high open woods, and was formerly found in great abundance in Ohio, Indiana, Kentucky, and West Virginia, but is now rare. Ginseng has also been hunted to near extinction in the wild.

Many medicines can be found in fields and forests if you know what to look for. Here are some common folk remedies:

Stop bleeding:

Dove's-foot/Crane's bill: Expressed juice.
Giant puffball: Packed as poultice.
Periwinkle: Expressed juice of leaves.
Plantains: Pounded leaves as poultice
Self-heal: Expressed juice
Stork's-bill: Expressed juice of leaves.
Woundwort: Expressed juice.

Cleansing rashes / sores / wounds:

Note: Use these plants externally to bathe the skin or where indicated as a poultice. Apply 2 or 3 times a day.
Burdock: Decoction of root, crushed raw root and salt for animal bites
Camomile: Infusion of flowers as poultice
Chickweed: Expressed juice of leaves
Cleavers: Infusion of whole plant except roots
Comfrey: Decoction of root as poultice
Nettle: Infusion of flowers and shoots.
Docks: Crushed leaves.
Elder: Expressed juice of leaves
Elm: Infusion of bark
Horehound: Infusion of whole plant except root
Mallow: Decoction of leaves and flowers as poultice
Marsh mallow: Decoction of root, infusion of leaves & flowers as poultice
Oak: Decoction of bark
Sanicle: Infusion of whole plant except root
Scurvy grass: Crushed leaves
Shepherd's purse: Infusion of whole plant but root as

poultice

Silverweed: Infusion of whole plant except root

Solomon's seal: Decoction of root as poultice

St. John wort: Infusion of flowers & shoots

Sorrel: Crushed leaves

Tansy: Crushed leaves

Watercress: Expressed juice

Woundwort: Infusion whole plant except roots

Yarrow: Infusion of whole plant but roots

Antiseptic:

Note: These plants can be used externally or internally. They are particularly useful for wounds that have become infected.

Garlic: Expressed juice

Mallow: Infusion of leaves and flowers

Marsh mallow: Decoction of root, infusion of flowers and leaves

Horseradish: Decoction of root

Thyme: Infusion of leaves and flowers

Ache / pains / bruises / stiffness:

Note: Where indicated use externally.

Balm: Infusion of leaves

Birch: Infusion of leaves

Borage: Infusion of whole plant, but roots

Burdock: Decoction of root

Camomile: Expressed juice of flowers applied to swelling

Chickenweed: Infusion of whole plant except root

Comfrey: Decoction of root applied to swelling

Cowberry: Infusion of leaves and fruits.

Dock: Crushed leaves applied to bruises

Dove's foot & crane's-bill: Infusion of whole plant but roots applied to swellings

Elm: Infusion of bark.

Figwort: Decoction of whole plant except root; use externally to draw bruises and blood clots.

Garlic: Expressed juice applied to swelling.

Remember especially for headache: Willow leaves and barks make a decoction containing salicin (a base for aspirin).

Fevers:

These plants will induce perspiration to break a fever.

Camomile: Infusion of leaves and flowers

Elder: Infusion of flowers and fruit

Elm: Decoction of bark

Feverfew: Infusion of whole plant except roots

Lime: Infusion of flowers.

Colds / sore throats / respiratory:

Agrimony: Infusion of whole plant but roots

Angelica: Decoction of root

Bilberry: Infusion of leaves and fruits

Bistort: Infusion of whole plant but roots

Borage: Infusion of whole plant except roots

Burdock: Decoction of roots.

Camomile: Infusion of flower use as gargle

Colt's foot: Infusion of leaves and flowers

Comfrey: Infusion of whole plant

Great mullein: Infusion of whole plant but roots, decoction of root as gargle.

Horehound: Infusion of whole plant but roots

Horseradish: Raw root

Lime: Infusion of flowers

Lungwort: Infusion of whole plant but roots.

Mallow: Infusion of flowers and leaves

Marshmallow: Decoction of root and infusion of leaves & flowers

Mint: Infusion of whole plant but roots

Mountain avens: Infusion of whole plant, use as gargle.

Nettle: Infusion of leaves

Oak: Decoction of bark; use as gargle

Plantain: Infusion of leaves and stems

Poplars: Infusion of leaves buds.
Rose: Decoction of hips
Sanicle: Infusion of whole plant but nut roots
Self-heal: Infusion of whole plant but roots, use as gargle.
St. John's wort: Infusion of flowers & shoots
Thyme: Infusion of leaves & flowers
Willow: Decoction of bark
Yarrow: Infusion of whole plant but roots use as inhalant.

Yarrow: Infusion of leaves and flowers

Diarrhoea:

Note: Take 2 or 3 times daily till symptoms subside.
Bilberry: Decoction of fruit
Bistort: Infusion of whole plant but roots
Bramble: Infusion of leaves or decoction of fruit
Cowberry: Decoction of fruit
Elm: Infusion of bark
Great burnet: Infusion of leaves and shoots

Hush Puppies (to deep fry)

Use the same dough as skillet corn bread (page 42), adding 1 teaspoon onion powder. Heat 2 cups canola oil in a deep pan until a small piece of dough dropped in sizzles a little. Shape dough into little balls, adding a little more flour if needed. Drop a few at a time into hot fat and cook until browned outside and cooked on the inside. Remove with a slotted spoon and drain on brown paper bags cut open.

Pancakes   12 to 16 hot cakes

2 cups flour
2 teaspoons baking powder
1/2 teaspoon salt
1 Tablespoon sugar
1 egg (optional)
2 Tablespoons canola oil
1 1/2 cups milk or water

Measure dry ingredients into a bowl. Add egg and liquids and stir just until mixed, batter may be lumpy. Heat a heavy pan or griddle, oil lightly and spoon on batter. Turn as soon as bubbles begin to form in pancake, cook other side. **Variation:** Add dried fruits or grated apple.

Settling stomach:

Balm: Infusion of leaves
Bilberry: Decoction of fruit
Bracken: Infusion of leaves
Dandelion: Decoction of whole plant.
Horseradish: Infusion of root
Mint: Infusion of whole plant but roots with crushed charcoal
Solomon's seal: Decoction of roots
Sanicle: Infusion of roots

Hazel: Infusion of leaves
Mint: Infusion of whole plant but roots
Mountain avens: Infusion of whole plants but roots
Oak: Decoction of bark
Plantain: Infusion of leaves and stems
Periwinkle: Infusion of leaves; not to use for long periods
Silverweed: Infusion of whole plant but roots.

Constipation:

Agrimony: Infusion of whole plant but roots
Barberry: Expressed juice of fruit
Common cleavers: Infusion of whole plant but roots
Couch grass: (Elymus): Decoction of root
Dandelion: Decoction of whole plant.
Elder: Expressed juice of fruit
Feverfew: Infusion of leaves and flowers
Rowan: Expressed juice of fruit
Rose: Decoction of hips
Walnut: Decoction of bark

Hemorrhoids:

Note: Apply externally 2 or 3 times a day.
Bilberry: Expressed juice of fruit
Camomile: Infusion of leaves and flowers
Elm: Decoction of bark

Lesser celandine: Expressed juice of leaves
Oak: Decoction of bark
Plantain: Expressed juice
Poplar: Decoction of leaf buds
Silverweed: Infusion of whole plant but root
Solomon's seal: Decoction of root.

Expelling worms:

Bracken: Infusion of root
Feverfew: Decoction leaves and flowers
Figwort: Infusion of whole plant but roots
Tansy: Infusion of leaves & flowers, use sparingly in small amount.

Burns:

For healing: Expressed the juice from comfrey leaves to aid tissue regrowth (cuts / burns).
Aloe: Salve of the jelly

"The world is working its way through a very difficult period.... The circumstances and issues are unprecedented, very complex. People who look for easy answers and guarantees are misguided. (These problems) do not lend themselves to black-and-white views."

Robert Rubin, Secretary of the Treasury,
Fortune Magazine, Sept. 28, 1998

Index

About the Authors

Dorothy R. Bates is a former home economist for the food industry and successful Realtor. Author of 9 books, she lives on a farm in rural Tennessee where she is developing sustainable agroforestry, conducting culinary workshops, and working part-time as an investment counselor. She is a member of the International Association of Culinary Professionals.

Albert K. Bates, the son of Dorothy Bates, is a retired public interest attorney and author of 6 books on energy, environment, and history. His textbook, *Climate in Crisis,* was listed among the best nonfiction works of 1990 by The Futurist Society. He currently travels, lecturing and teaching permaculture and village design for the Global Ecovillage Network.

Books by Dorothy R. Bates

How to Run a Real Estate Office
The New Farm Vegetarian Cookbook
The Tempeh Cookbook
The Seitan Cookbook
The TVP Cookbook
Kids Can Cook!
The George Bernard Shaw Vegetarian Cookbook
The Holiday Diet Cookbook
Eat Cheaply!

Books by Albert K. Bates

The Grass Case
Honicker v. Hendrie, A Lawsuit to End Atomic Power
Shutdown! Nuclear Power on Trial
Your Rights to Victims Compensation
Climate in Crisis: The Greenhouse Effect and What We Can Do